The Fatherhood of God
in an Age of
Emancipation

Books by W. A. Visser 't Hooft
Published by The Westminster Press

The Fatherhood of God in an Age of Emancipation
Memoirs
No Other Name
Rembrandt and the Gospel
The Renewal of the Church

W.A. Visser't Hooft

The Fatherhood of God in an Age of Emancipation

The Westminster Press
Philadelphia

© 1982 World Council of Churches

Published by The Westminster Press®
Philadelphia, Pennsylvania

PRINTED IN THE UNITED STATES OF AMERICA
9 8 7 6 5 4 3 2 1

Library of Congress Cataloging in Publication Data

Visser 't Hooft, Willem Adolph, 1900-
    The fatherhood of God in an age of emancipation.

    Includes bibliographical references.
    1. God—Fatherhood.   I. Title.
BT153.F3V57 1983   261.1   82-13403
ISBN 0-664-24462-9 (pbk.)

To Margaret Kooijman
whose help and advice have been so precious
that my book has become our book

Contents

Preface

One of the few advantages of old age is that it provides an opportunity to satisfy one's intellectual curiosity in a way that was not possible in earlier years. At last it is possible to dive into that great ocean of books which one's other duties had always prevented one from reading.

In my case, these are principally books on the history of ideas, especially those dealing with the relationship between culture and religion. The more I read, the more I ask myself whether our modern cultural history has any recognizable pattern. Is it true that, in our times, history is essentially that of the emancipation of humankind from patriarchal and authoritarian conceptions of life and society? Then there is the next question: "If emancipation is inevitable, does it mean that the fatherhood of God is becoming an anachronism? Is it a hopeless task to speak of God the Father to men and women for whom fatherhood has no great value, or even calls up negative associations?"

I searched for books which dealt specifically with these questions but did not find what I sought. So I began to make notes on the subject, based both on my reading and on my experiences during many years and in many countries. In arranging these notes, I found that I had the outline of a book. And so I began to write it and the labour it involved was the punishment for my curiosity.

I am of course aware that I do not have a specialist's knowledge in the seven or eight areas of life with which this book is concerned, but since today no one can be a specialist in more than one field, 'generalists' must participate in the discussion necessary to allow us to plan for the future.

The story of emancipation as I have described it is of course not the whole story. I am particularly conscious that I have not dealt adequately with the process of emancipation in Asia, Africa and Latin America. I have written something about emancipation from colonialism, but have barely touched upon the other acute problems which arise as new generations in these continents seek to liberate themselves from patriarchal elements in their own cultures.

Some of my readers may feel that I have not given sufficient attention to the technical and psychological aspects of the problem. My excuse is that I cannot find my way about the labyrinth of psychological schools and theories. I hope, however, that psychological judgment of a non-technical nature is not wholly absent from these pages.

As my explanation of the origin of this book suggests, my purpose, in the first place, is to meet the challenge of the 'society without fathers', the arrival of which has been announced by Alexander Mitscherlich and a number of other sociologists and historians of ideas. The major part of my book had already been written before I came across Mary Daly's *Beyond God the Father — Toward a Philosophy of Women's Liberation,* an influential book dealing with the subject from a very different angle. That exercise in iconoclasm is certainly a landmark in the history of emancipation, but it forms only part of that history and does not, as it announces, provide a definitive solution to the problem. Sexism is certainly a powerful cause of oppression, but it is not 'the final cause.'[1] I do not believe that all oppression and domination would cease if sexism were overcome, because the end cause of oppression is not the wrong attitude of one human group to another; it is rooted in the hearts of all human beings. My book does not, therefore, seek to react against radical or any other kind of feminism; it only strives to place this very urgent issue in a wider context.

I am writing at a time when battles for various kinds of emancipation are raging fiercely. On the one side are the vast multitudes of the oppressed who have become acutely aware of the injustice of their fate: the poor who see no improvement ahead, the victims of racism and dictatorship, those women who are still treated as inferior beings, the young who feel that they are not being given a chance, the church members whose voices are not heard by their

---

[1]Mary Daly, *Beyond God the Father — Toward a Philosophy of Women's Liberation,* Boston, Beacon Press, 1973, p. 180.

leaders. The anger of such groups frequently takes wild and irresponsible forms, and their dreams of what will follow emancipation are often so Utopian that they can lead only to disappointment. But to be deaf to their cries is to forget that the human spirit cannot be permanently broken, and these voices demand to be heard.

On the other side are those whose chief concern is to defend the cohesion of society and the validity of traditional norms. They are of the opinion that any revolt against authoritarianism will open the door for anarchy, and their distrust of the increasing permissiveness in society and the disintegration which is its consequence must be taken seriously. However, movements like those of the 'moral majority' and the 'neo-conservatives', and the ideological orthodoxy of the left or the right, all of which strive to hold back the waves of emancipation for the sake of maintaining the present order, can only deepen the anger of the partisans of change. Both those who conceive of emancipation as a panacea and those who see it as a dangerous disease are leading us into blind alleys.

It is time to call out: *Tertium datur* — there is a third way.

It is time to ask if true emancipation is not that found by the prodigal son when he returned to his father's house — a house where, because of the love which it contained, order was not domination, nor freedom anarchy.

Geneva   October 1981

1. The issue

Among the many graffiti written on the walls of the Sorbonne in the wild summer of 1968 when the students rose in revolt against the established order of things, none explained better what they had in mind than: "Unless emancipation is total, it is not real emancipation." The students were not speaking only for themselves. Their slogan expressed a deep and powerful trend in the cultural history of the Western world.

Sociologists had already begun to analyse that trend, and some of them had come to the conclusion, as Alexander Mitscherlich put it, that we were "on the way to a fatherless society". The structures of the old society dependent upon the authoritarian father had broken down. Dietrich Bonhoeffer, in his prison cell, had arrived at a similar conclusion. During recent centuries, the world had come of age. This adult world no longer felt the need of any form of tutelage. It was very conscious of its emancipated status and believed that it could live without a guardian God.

It is clear that this has created an entirely new situation for the Christian church. Throughout its history, it had been concerned with civilizations which were deeply influenced by patriarchal traditions and had, to a considerable extent, absorbed these traditions into its own life. Now it had to be asked how the church could render its witness in a post-patriarchal world.

Yet the witness of the church is a message about Jesus Christ as the Son of God the Father. It is at the same time a message about the nature of God's fatherly love for people. We cannot eliminate fatherhood from the gospel without destroying its very meaning. On the other hand, could children, growing up in a society in which fathers were less and less respected and played a decreasingly important role, be expected to respond to such a message? Would they not perforce come to the conclusion that this message was an anachronism which belonged to the past, with the father role of authoritarian rulers or autocratic heads of families?

2. Emancipation

To find answers to these questions, we must first seek to understand the nature of the process of emancipation during the last centuries, which is still going on today. At the present time, the term 'emancipation' is used in a number of different ways, indicating liberation from the domination of economic, political or natural forces, and even from earlier ideas, customs and moral standards. In its original form in Roman law, however, it meant the transition from the position in which one was wholly dependent on the *patria potestas* of one's father to that in which one was *sui juris*, or independent, and therefore able to function oneself as *pater familias*, as the head of a family.

I shall use the term 'emancipation' in this basic meaning, for I am not writing about liberation in general, but about that specific form of liberation which is emancipation from patriarchal modes of living and thinking. This does not mean that I shall follow a narrow path, but rather the contrary, for the patriarchal spirit and the doctrine upon which it is based have had an astonishingly wide influence, penetrating into many different spheres of life. Indeed, it has not been merely one of many facets of society, but has rather formed its general pattern. When we speak of emancipation from paternalism, therefore, we have to consider not only developments in family life, but also those in the state, the church and even in international relations.

We shall find that there is great variety in these struggles for emancipation. Some develop very slowly while others have had an explosive character. Some have met with fierce opposition — others have won their victories easily. There is no regular pattern and no uniformity in their development. One of the reasons for this is that the struggle for emancipation has generally been fought against one particular form of domination or oppression and not against domination or oppression in general. Emancipation as a concept for long remained abstract, food for philosophers but not for the masses. It was easier for the leaders of struggles for emancipation to win support if public attention were focused on concrete abuses such as absolute monarchy, slavery or the glaring inequality between men and women. Looking back on the whole development, it is sometimes amusing, and sometimes irritating, to note that those who fought for emancipation in one area of life were often totally blind to oppression in other, no less vital, parts of society. There have been great prophets of revolution against tyranny in the state who did not lift a finger in protest against tyranny in the family. Great protagonists of the emancipation of dependent peoples have refused to recognize the right of workers to fight for greater economic freedom.

It may, at this point, be asked whether a man who has not himself gone through the painful, costly though exhilarating process of emancipation is qualified to deal with this subject. I have never suffered greatly from patriarchalism. In my family there was an atmosphere of considerable freedom. I belong to the sex which has so far been dominating rather than dominated. My country has a monarchy, but it is a constitutional monarchy from which most Dutchmen neither need nor want to be liberated. With regard to the colonial situation, we were the colonizers and not the colonized. Really to understand what it means to throw off the yoke of patriarchal domination, one has to turn to the writings of those who devoted their lives to the struggle for freedom.

In spite of that, I believe that a man in my position can make some contribution to the study of this subject. I was born in 1900, and therefore belong to a generation which knew the patriarchal world before it was transformed and which has yet lived to see emancipation taking place in more areas and with greater speed than at any other time in history. Mine is thus a typical generation of transition from one stage of cultural history to another.

I may add that through my international work, and the travel which it involved, I was able to get into personal touch with many emancipation movements and their representatives in different parts of the world. My knowledge of these movements is thus not based on books and documents only, but also on direct encounter with the men and women who were deeply involved in these struggles. My first task, however, is to analyse the character and strength of that patriarchalism against which the modern world has so sharply revolted.

3. The weight of patriarchal tradition

How deeply Western civilization has been influenced by the traditions of patriarchalism may be measured in a number of ways. Let us start by comparing the role of the father in Ancient Israel and in Rome, two societies which have left a greater mark on life in the West as it is today than any other.

There is a remarkable resemblance between the patterns of these two worlds. In both, the family was the basic unit of society, dominated by the father, under the paternal roof. The father's role was monarchal, and the principal duty of the children was to honour and obey him. In Israel, the father was also the judge and priest of the household, holding social and religious sway over his wife or wives, his children and his slaves. His power was absolute, and he could, if he so desired, sell his daughter into slavery.[1] In Rome, the father had many of the same prerogatives and his *patria potestas* had the unique feature that it continued to operate as long as he lived. In other words, his son could not become a *persona seus juris,* a free person under the law, until his father died, or decided to emancipate him.

In both societies, the wife was in a position of subordination to her husband. In the Israel of the Old Testament, the husband was to his wife 'baal', that is lord. Both there and in Rome, the wife's behaviour was much more strictly regulated than was that of her husband. She could, however, have a very important role in the family. It was not only the father, but the father and mother together who were entitled to respect. The wife, however, and indeed all the women of the household, held a position inferior to that of the *pater familias* and had to obey him.

The original form of government in both societies was government by the elders. In Israel, the elders were associated with Moses when he went to the Holy Mountain to receive the Tables of the Law and this gerontocracy survived in one form or another throughout the history of the people. In the time of the Maccabees, there was still a *gerousia,* or council of elders. Although it was inevitable that these councils should come to include men who did not yet belong to the older generation, the theory remained that only the elders had the experience and wisdom necessary for leading the people. In Rome, the members of the Senate were called 'the fathers', "both because the Senate had first been made up of old men and also because it was their duty and office to have a fatherly care of the commonwealth. To which you may add: because the name of father carried with it veneration, love and respect."[2]

In both cultures, tradition played a decisive role. The poet Ennius said of Rome: *Moribus antiquis stat res Romana virisque* — "Rome stands or falls by its ancient customs and its men." The spiritual leaders of Israel exhorted the people to live "according to the tradition of the elders".[3] But tradition has to be constantly revitalized by commemoration. It is well-known that today the Jews continue to celebrate the central event of their history by a family meal, where psalms are sung and the story of the Exodus is recalled. Now it is remarkable that Horace's description of the festivals of a Roman family contains many of the same features. He says in his *Odes*[4] that the Romans, with their wives and children, "having first solemnly invoked the gods, celebrate after the manner of our ancestors, joining our voice to the flute, our great Captains renowned for their virtue." He goes on: "We will sing of Troy, of Anchises and the progeny of beauteous Venus," in reference to the story of the birth of Aeneas and the origins of Rome. Thus the patriarchal system received its religious sanction. The father was the priest in his own home. *Pietas,* which means at the same time the respect of children for their parents and the reverence due to the gods, became deified and was worshipped in a special temple in Rome. In Israel, the commandment to honour one's father and mother was not only one of the ten revealed to Moses but was also the subject of constant meditation in the Wisdom Literature. In the Jewish liturgy, many prayers begin with the words: "Yahveh our God and the God of our Fathers."

Horace speaks of the Roman Senate as *patrum sanctum concilium*[5] and it is interesting and significant that the holy council of fathers which we think of today in connection with Rome, the Vatican Council, bears the same name.

But was this tenacious patriarchal tradition not abolished by Christianity? The answer, I believe, is that it was not done away with, but changed, as I shall explain more fully later in this study. For the moment, I shall say only that, in the life and teaching of Jesus, fatherhood became the central concept in descriptions of God's dealings with people; but, precisely because God's fatherhood now became dominant, human fatherhood took second place. Jesus brought a new sense of proportion, so that the claims of God the Father in Heaven took precedence over any claim made by human fathers. The norms of the patriarchal society were not denied, but they lost their absolute character and their immutability and were no longer a prison. Those who followed Jesus and became children of God were free, emancipated men and women.

St Paul preached the same message of liberation, that Christ had set us free by enabling us to be adopted as sons of God. In some of the young churches however, as we read in the Epistles, this new freedom was misconstrued as an invitation to unlimited self-indulgence and the denial of moral standards and social conventions. Paul reacted by again placing greater emphasis on the need to follow the rules of the patriarchal world.

The young church thus lived in tension between the old patriarchal ethic and the claims of the new faith. Christian martyrs chose to obey God, even if this meant disobedience to parents, husbands, or the civil authorities, and this led in many cases to tragedy.

The situation changed radically of course in the fourth century AD when, under Constantine the Great, the church ceased to be a persecuted minority, and Christianity became the official religion of the Roman Empire. As St Augustine said, this happened 'extremely fast'. There was no time for the church to work out a new social system inspired by the Christian faith. The line of least resistance was therefore chosen, and the church by and large accepted the existing social framework, so that inevitably the patriarchal system remained in force.

The patriarchal tradition was transmitted to Western civilization through three main channels. Of great importance was the channel of Roman law, which has continued to influence life until the present day. When the Eastern Emperor Justinian, who greatly desired to restore and strengthen his Christian Empire, sought a well-defined legal system, he ordered his jurists to codify the laws of the Roman Empire. It is true that, on the basis of Christian insights, a number of modifications were made, and some of the more rigorous rules relating to *patria potestas* were mitigated, but the *Corpus Juris Civilis,* the Justinian Code, remains basically a product of Roman thought rather than of Christian insight.

Another important channel of transmission was, of course, the Old Testament. In spite of attempts made by Marcion and certain gnostic sects to present the Christian faith as opposed to, rather than rooted in, the revelation to Israel, the church defended the validity of the Old Testament. Its teaching, passed on through writing, preaching, religious art, and in other ways, was interpreted not as history but as a source of moral example, directly applicable to the lives of Christians in the Middle Ages.

As indicated above, however, the most important means by which the patriarchal ethos was passed on was the church itself, as it became more and more a typical patriarchal institution. The bishop, the father of his flock, became the central figure in church organization. Also in its attitude to women, the church followed the patriarchal line. They had no voice in church affairs. The hierarchical structure found its head in the Pope, the father *par excellence,* and obedience to the hierarchical superior became one of the main virtues.

In the realm of theology, we again find that the interrelated authority of the *pater familias,* and of the magistrate or ruler, became recognized aspects of the order of society, regarded as divinely instituted. This theme dominated the teaching of theologians and church leaders throughout the centuries.

According to St Augustine the family was of prime importance as the place where people lived together in orderly relations of command and obedience. He stressed, however, that in Christian families the husbands, masters though they were, should regard themselves as the servants of those they commanded, for they had to rule, not with the pride of a sovereign but with the mercy of a provider. St Augustine saw this as the model to be followed in society, and in the commonwealth.

> The ordered harmony of authority and obedience between those who live together has a relation to the ordered harmony of authority

and obedience between those who live in a city. This explains why a father must apply certain regulations of civil law to the governance of his home, so as to make it accord with the peace of the whole community.[6]

The same idea is to be found in the writings of Thomas Aquinas, who said: "He who rules in the home is not called king, but *pater familias,* but he has something in common with a king, for kings are sometimes called fathers of their people."[7]

The Reformers followed the tradition thus set for them by their predecessors. They gave patriarchal authority a strong basis by interpreting the commandment to honour father and mother as referring to all relationships with those in authority. In his Great Catechism, Luther enumerates four categories of people who should be honoured: parents, heads of families, magistrates and pastors. He stated that God had given the highest status to parents, who represented him on earth, so that paternal authority was the foundation of all human relations.

With regard to rulers and magistrates, the Great Catechism recalled that people in ancient times had called their rulers *patres patriae,* 'fathers of the fatherland', and called upon Christians to honour them, using for them the same title. On the other hand, Luther stressed that those in authority had to remember that they had not been granted power for their own glorification, and that, in obedience to God, they had to care for the spiritual and material needs of their subjects.

Calvin agreed with Luther, and stressed in his turn that the commandment to honour father and mother was a universal rule, calling upon us to honour, revere and love all those ordained as our superiors. It was not for us to question whether our superiors were worthy of that honour, for they had been placed above us by the will of God. If, on the other hand, these superiors tried to force us to violate the law of God, they must be treated as strangers who desired to turn us away from our true Father.[8] Further, according to the Second Helvetic Confession of 1566, God has given the magistrate or civil authority to the world as a kind of father *(veluti patrem)* and the faithful must therefore honour, love, aid and pray for him as for a father.

No further examples are needed. It is clear that, in particular through the teaching of all the main churches, generation after generation was presented with the patriarchal ideal as the ultimate ideal of society.

But was it really an ideal, or rather a mask behind which great vested interests hid themselves? There are many today who hate patriarchalism so violently that they cannot believe that honest men and women ever held it as a worthy ideal. Yet could so many people of all classes have accepted for so long a system that was wholly inimical to people? Must we reject as hypocritical servants of the established order all the great teachers who have defended patriarchalism? Was patriarchalism always and totally wrong?

It is obvious that in many cases it has led to very wrong actions. When St Augustine urged the civil authorities to use coercion against the Donatist heretics, his main argument was that here must be applied the discipline which fathers ought to use in their families. There are innumerable later occasions when harsh treatment of dependents or dependent peoples has been defended on the same grounds. There is, however, another side to the coin. At its best, patriarchal society is one held together by personal relations of responsibility and loyalty which provide for people great spiritual and material security.

In our consideration of the great historical struggle between patriarchalism and emancipation, therefore, we must not behave as partisans. I hope to make it clear that I believe in the necessity of emancipation, but that does not mean that I consider the patriarchal system to have been wrong at all times and in all circumstances, nor that I find every form of emancipation good.

How inadequate it is to adopt a one-sided view of great historical events can be illustrated by the reaction of two Englishmen to the French Revolution. Dr Richard Price was a dissenting minister of religion in London who believed whole-heartedly in the rights of men as defined by the French philosophers and was therefore in favour of all movements towards emancipation, even supporting Mary Wollstonecraft as one of the first feminists. In 1789, when the French Revolution broke out, Dr Price, in a sermon, expressed thankfulness that he had witnessed this event. He added: "I could almost say, 'Lord, now lettest Thou Thy servant depart in peace, for mine eyes have seen Thy salvation.' I have lived to see a diffusion of knowledge which has undermined superstition and error. I have lived to see the rights of men better understood than ever and nations panting for liberty which seemed to have lost the idea of it.

I have lived to see thirty millions of people, indignant and resolute, spurning at slavery and demanding liberty with an irresistible voice, their king led in triumph, as an arbitrary monarch surrendering himself to his subjects."

When the famous statesman, Edmund Burke, heard of this sermon, he became indignant and wrote his well-known *Reflections on the French Revolution,* in which he took a position directly opposed to that of Price. For him, the French Revolution denied and destroyed all the customs and institutions which he held dear. The social order attacked by the revolutionaries had had its origin in that ancient chivalry which was characterized by the spirit of 'fealty' and created love, veneration and attachment between people. Burke questioned whether this system, which had given Europe its special place in the world, must now be abolished. "Never, never more shall we behold that generous loyalty to rank and sex, that proud submission, that dignified obedience, that subordination of the heart which kept alive, even in servitude itself, the spirit of an exalted freedom..." ... "The age of chivalry is gone. That of sophisters, economists and calculators has succeeded; and the glory of Europe is extinguished for ever."

These two judgments both show an incapacity on the part of their authors to recognize the ambivalent character of great historical upheavals. Dr Price could not have shouted 'Hallelujah' without reserve if he had reflected upon the collapse of values and the new violence which the Revolution would bring in its wake. Burke could not have condemned it so absolutely if he had given more thought to the oppressive features of the old patriarchal world, or listened more attentively to voices clamouring for a true emancipation of people.

That it is possible to arrive at a more generous, less one-sided, and therefore more realistic judgment is shown by the position taken by Dietrich Bonhoeffer. He came from a family which, according to his brother Klaus, had 'a patriarchal constitution'[9] and he had a strong attachment to the traditions of his country and his milieu. "To be deeply rooted in the soil of the past makes life harder, but it also makes it richer and more vigorous. There are in human life certain fundamental truths to which men will always return sooner or later." [10] Bonhoeffer was, at the same time, deeply conscious that a new type of human being was appearing, the modern adult person, one who wanted to use one's own powers of reason and to stand on one's own feet. He was thus able to see both the danger and the promise in the great emancipation movements. For him, as stated in his *Ethics*, the French Revolution had indeed liberated people, though he recognized that if you made of freedom an absolute idea, this could lead to nihilism. Yet such a struggle had been inevitable and had to be accepted as a historical necessity.

4. Emancipation from the domination of patriarchal rulers

My first impression of the vicissitudes of world history came in 1910, when I learned as a schoolboy that the King of Portugal had been driven from his throne. That kings could be dismissed in this way was a shocking discovery. Brought up to have a firm attachment to the House of Orange, I had believed monarchs to be the incarnation of stability and the guardians of the established order.

Let us therefore look at the rise and fall of patriarchal rule, not only of rule by monarchs, but all authoritarian rule, as it has been until our day.

The title 'father of the fatherland' — *pater patriae* — has been used so often in poems, addresses of welcome and obituaries that it has lost its significance. There was a time, however, when it had deep meaning. Suetonius tells us that when the Roman Senate decided to confer this title on Augustus, he replied with tears: "Fathers of the Senate, I have at last achieved my highest ambition. What more can I ask of the immortal gods than that they may permit me to enjoy your approval until my dying day."[1] Why, it may be asked, was Augustus so deeply moved? It would seem that the title *pater familias* expressed that complete confidence which a respectful son should have in his father. To accept the title therefore meant to accept a tremendous responsibility. Tiberius, the successor of Augustus, indeed refused the title, according to Suetonius, "for fear that his shame would be intensified when he turned out to be unworthy of such an honour."[2]

Throughout the following centuries, the paternal authority of monarchs and other absolute rulers continued to be accepted as right. In all the main Christian traditions, respect for and obedience to royal authority were based on the commandment to honour father and mother.

In the seventeenth century, however, the fatherhood of the ruler became a subject of passionate controversy, and, as most states were then ruled by absolute monarchs, it was this form of rule which was brought into question.

The doctrine of royal fatherhood had still its enthusiastic defenders. In England, Sir Robert Filmer's book with the significant title *Patriarcha* had a great success and was reprinted many times. It supported the divine right of kings and the necessity of an absolute monarchy, and was, as John Locke complained, "the current divinity of the times" — the theory preached by most theologians.

Sir Robert's theory was amazingly simple. Adam had had unlimited power over his wife and children and kings were the heirs of Adam. They had therefore 'sovereignty by fatherhood' over their subjects and passed this on to their heirs by "the ancient and prime right of lineal succession to paternal government." Resistance to the monarch was always a breach of the clear commandment to honour father and mother.

John Locke, the philosopher, whose point of departure was the inherent freedom of persons and who had therefore chosen to support William III and Mary against James II, considered Sir Robert Filmer's doctrine very dangerous, for it could have undermined the position of William. If the author of *Patriarcha* was right, William's operation was not a Glorious Revolution but an infamous rebellion. In order, therefore, "to establish the throne of our great restorer" and "to make good his title in the consent of the people", Locke wrote his *Two Treatises on Government* (1690). The first was an extremely effective criticism of *Patriarcha*. In relation to our subject, it is of great importance that Locke made clear that there was a fundamental difference between paternal power and governmental power, between the authority of the father and that of the king. According to him, the power of the father was patriarchal but limited in time and extent. That of the king was not patriarchal because it was based on a contractual relationship. Absolute monarchy was wrong, because it eliminated the right of appeal to laws by which the monarch was bound. Resistance to tyranny was necessary when royal power became tyrannical.

Locke's book was the most thoughtful and effective criticism of royal fatherhood which had yet appeared. It is therefore not astonishing that it had widespread influence, for example in France, on the thinking of Montesquieu, and in the United States of America, on the drafters of the Bill of Rights.

At this time France, under Louis XIV, was the perfect example of an absolute monarchy. The man who provided the theory on which this was built was the theologian Bossuet, who sought also to pass his convictions on to the Grand Dauphin, Louis's eldest son. His theory was less extreme than that of Filmer, but it also was definitely patriarchal. His conception of government was "the policy drawn from the words of the Holy Scriptures." Paternal authority paved the way for royal authority, and people thus became accustomed to obey one single chief. Royal authority was sacred, paternal and absolute, but it had to be applied with reason. On the other hand, although the king had to rule his subjects in a reasonable way, he was not responsible to them, and they had to obey without argument, and must never resist the government.[3]

Louis XIV was in complete agreement with Bossuet's ideal of paternalistic kingship. In a letter written at the end of his life to the great-grandson who succeeded him, he said: "Set your subjects the same example as a Christian father sets his family. Consider them as your children, make them happy, if you want to be happy your-self."[4]

Both Louis XIV and Bossuet, however, lived long enough to experience very disturbing signs of a great change in the spiritual and political climate. The great "crisis of the European con-science" had arrived. Bossuet had been horrified by Spinoza's attack on the divine right of kings, and when a leading Huguenot theologian, Jurieu, advocated armed resistance against the King of France, Bossuet replied that it had become clear to him that the Reformation was not Christian, for it was not faithful to its royal overlord and to its fatherland. Bossuet saw the great danger to be 'the intemperance of the spirit' and "a pride which cannot accept its remedy, namely a legitimate authority."[5]

The conception of the royal father had lost much of its force, as was seen in Britain by the execution of King Charles I. It survived through the eighteenth century, but as a flower cut from its roots. Voltaire, the sceptic, could write about the relationship between kings and their subjects:

Ils sont tous ses enfants: cette famille immense
Dans ses soins paternels a mis sa confiance.[6]

People were reaching a stage of development in which they were no longer willing to be treated as children, and this led to the explosion of the French Revolution. It was a wild attempt to prove that men and women had really come of age and that they were the artisans of their own fate. The era of fathers as rulers had ended, and to make this crystal clear the king, who had been the incarnation of paternalism, had not only to be dethroned, but even to be killed. It is not easy for us today to understand the cheers of triumph which were raised, not only in France but also in many other places, when the king was brought to the guillotine. They were the cheers of people who naively believed that the era of total emancipation had arrived.

This was however not yet the end of royal fatherhood. After the Napoleonic intermezzo, the cry was for the restoration of royal paternalism. Czar Alexander I of Russia took the initiative in the formation of the Holy Alliance of Russia, Austria and Prussia, in which the sovereigns declared that "in line with the words of Holy Scripture, they will consider themselves with regard to their subjects and armies as fathers of their family." This treaty has often been described as an extraordinary piece of hypocrisy. Shelley wrote so violently against it that his publisher did not dare to print the passage. In the preface to his poem "Hellas", Shelley wrote: "This is the age of the war of the oppressed against the oppressors and every one of those ringleaders of the privileged gangs of murderers and swindlers, called Sovereigns, looks to each other for aid against the common enemy, and suspends their mutual jealousies in the presence of a mightier fear. Of this Holy Alliance all the despots of the earth are virtual members." Even the men mainly responsible for carrying out the policies of the Holy Alliance, in particular Metternich and von Gentz, made cynical remarks about it. I do not believe however that the Christian Europe of Alexander's ideal, living piously and in great tranquillity under the watchful tutelage of benevolent fatherly rulers, was nothing but a facade. The idea arose from his Russian mysticism, and the pietism which he had learned from Madame de Krüdener, a Russian society woman who claimed prophetic powers and had gained a great influence over the Czar's religious life. The patriarchal system established by the Holy Alliance could not have maintained itself for so many decades had it not found strong defenders deeply convinced that it was right. Even in France, there were enthusiastic prophets of patriarchalism, like de Maistre, and Louis de Bonald who coined the remarkable formula: "Society is paternity and dependence, far more than equality and fraternity." Yet the opposition was increasing in strength. The change in the intellectual climate is illustrated by the life story of the Abbé de Lamennais who, in his early days, was hailed as a second Bossuet but who later broke with Rome and became a zealous apostle of liberty. In his *Livre du Peuple* he wrote: "They have said that the royal power was that of a father over children who are always under age and under guardianship. Therefore the people have no freedom and no property and are eternally incapable of judging what is good and what is bad, useful or not, and so they live in a total dependence on the prince who deals with them in all matters according to his desires."

An even more effective weapon in the fight against patriarchal rulers was ridicule, and the master of ridicule was Heinrich Heine. In one of his *Zeitgedichte* (Poems of the Time), he said of the thirty-six kings, dukes and princes who ruled their territories within Germany that the people called them father and their lands fatherland, while also liking sauerkraut and sausage, and goes on to report that the rulers are greeted with respect, because Germany is a pious nursery and not a Roman den of cut-throats.[7]

The great clash between the protagonists of royal fatherhood and the pioneers of emancipation took place in 1848, when revolutions broke out all over Europe. At first it seemed as if the cause of freedom might be victorious. The man who had for so long been the incarnation of patriarchalism, Metternich, was forced to resign. In spite of this, the forces of conservatism proved too strong. The patriarchal system had lost much of its prestige but it was not yet beaten. In Berlin, where the populace had constructed barricades in the streets, the King of Prussia appealed to them: "Hear the fatherly words of your King, inhabitants of my loyal and beautiful Berlin, and forget what has happened as I shall forget it." In most countries, life soon resumed its normal course, but revolutionaries at home and in exile continued to plan change.

The country where the doctrine of the fatherhood of the ruler had its deepest roots was of course Russia. The Czar was the ruling father *par excellence* who was recognized in Western Europe, with praise or criticism, as the foremost defender of authoritarianism. Even there, however, history did not stand still, and questions began to be asked. Among the first to express new and dangerous thoughts was Dostoevsky. For this, he was condemned to death in 1850, though he was later pardoned and permitted to live. Towards the end of his life, he came to take a very different attitude to the monarchy, believing that Russia had a mission to create a new society by spreading the doctrine of Czarism. The new world of freedom would have as its only foundation "the filial love of the people for the Czar as for its father. For you can allow subjects who are treated as children many things which are unthinkable in nations where the people live according to laws. For children will not betray their father."[8] But, although Dostoevsky began by criticizing the imperial claim to universal fatherhood, and ended by defending it fervently, the main intellectual movement of his time was going in the opposite direction and the story of the relationship between the Czar and his people became increasingly tragic.

This historical review has brought us back to the twentieth century, and to the astonishment of a Dutch schoolboy at the abdication of the King of Portugal. The following years were to see the end of many further monarchies and, within the life-span of my generation, six empires and some ten kingdoms adopted a republican form of government.

The royal houses which survived were those which, seeing the signs of the times, had adapted their ways. Their subjects were free citizens, protected by law and owing loyal affection to monarchs whose power was constitutionally limited. All this was true of the Netherlands where, in addition, the House of Orange owed its origin to a man, William the Silent, who had won his place as father of his country by fighting foreign oppression, in fact against the established patriarchal order of his times, and his exploits are still proudly celebrated in the Netherlands National Anthem.

The monarchies that fell were thus those which had maintained a patriarchal ideology and form of government, those which had refused to realize that their subjects had grown up and were no longer prepared to submit to patriarchal domination. The kings and emperors who fell were not necessarily morally inferior to their predecessors, or to those who survived. Indeed, those whom I met, before or after their abdication, seemed to be men with a deep concern for the welfare of their peoples. The change was in the peoples who, awakening to their own adulthood, found a continuation of unquestioning obedience to an absolute ruler intolerable.

5. Emancipation from the master-servant relationship

Few social changes have been as complete as that which has overtaken the relationship of master and domestic servant in the recent past. Indeed, not many young people today have had any experience of this social custom, and the idea that one section of society should serve another in this way has become outdated. My generation however remembers the time when the employment of domestic servants was the rule rather than the exception, in households ranging from those of the rich and powerful to very simple bourgeois establishments. The distinction between master and servant was a fact of everyday life, and this situation had many patriarchal features, reaching far back into history.

Domestic life in the Ancient World was of course based largely on slavery. Domestic or house slaves, however, enjoyed a privileged position compared to others who worked as labourers, in mines, or even as gladiators in Roman circuses. The Christian belief that all men were equal before God, although it was an early step in at least the spiritual emancipation of persons born or sold into servitude, was not widely applied to their place in an earthly society.

A later stage, which lasted well into the Middle Ages, was that of serfdom. Serfs, although not in personal bondage, were tied to the land on which they were born, and there served their feudal masters. Flight availed them nothing, as no new master would accept their labour, but merely returned them to their starting point in the interest of keeping the system intact.

The force which finally emancipated serfs in most Western European countries was not a movement of liberation but a terrible pestilence, the Black Death or bubonic plague, which in the fourteenth century so decimated the working population that serfs, leaving their masters, were welcomed and paid wages by other land-owners desperate for labour to till their fields. Although serfdom came to an end in many countries at that time, it lasted in other places very much longer. In Russia, there was still serfdom in the nineteenth century, as we can learn from Gogol's great novel, *Dead Souls*.

Throughout the centuries, and parallel with slavery, free men and women had also worked as domestic servants. Some worked in large and distinguished establishments. When my wife's uncle, the Governor General of the Netherlands East Indies, was asked how many servants he had, he replied "between three and four hundred". At the other end of the scale would be found simple bourgeois households with one domestic servant, bullied or cherished according to the character of the master, or more probably of the mistress of the house. In larger establishments, the servants had a hierarchy of their own, in which the senior servants were themselves father figures for their juniors, and exercised an autocratic rule perhaps even more severe than did the masters.

It is clear that there was an evil side to this custom. Arbitrary or cruel masters exploited or ill-treated their servants, who, in their turn, lacked freedom to live as they chose, and possibly also economic freedom to leave their employment.

There was however also much that was positive in the system. Older people can remember servants, or even generations of servants of the same family, who remained with the same household for many years, and came to share a common life, in which the master displayed a great sense of responsibility for the wellbeing of his dependents and the servants assimilated themselves into the family, making its interests their own and playing an important part in the education of the master's children. The most extreme example of this type of cohesion which I have experienced was when I was staying at the same castle in Germany as Princess von Wied who, for a few months in 1914, had been Queen of Albania, and heard her manservant begin a story with the words: "When we ascended the Albanian throne..."

Various factors combined to bring about the emancipation of domestic servants, none of them, though, a deliberate movement to that end. Two world wars changed the face of society, leaving few families with sufficient income to maintain large establishments and to employ servants. In the war of 1914-1918, the almost total mobilization of young and middle-aged men in the belligerent countries forced, or permitted, women to leave domestic service for other work and this widening of opportunity for women has continued ever since until today women play important and responsible parts in all spheres of life. Thus domestic service faded away and with it departed both the good and the bad aspects of this manifestation of patriarchalism.

We must now examine the other form of master-servant relationship which is represented by the employer and the worker, which has also undergone great changes in the past hundred years.

In the apparently stable bourgeois society of the nineteenth and early twentieth centuries, the increasing strength of the socialist movement was considered by many as a dangerous development which should be energetically resisted. When in 1918 there were revolutionary stirrings in the Netherlands, students sided as a matter of course with the authorities. For my own part, it was only through my international contacts in the following years that I began to see socialism in a different light. In England, I learned much from the Quakers at their centre in Woodbrooke, and listened to the words of Bernard Shaw. At international student conferences, I met young people who were actively working for socialism and soon learned that most of the prophetic thinkers of the time were socialists of one kind or another. Karl Barth and Eduard Thurneysen, Nicolas Berdyaev and Paul Tillich, Reinhold Niebuhr, William Temple and André Philip — these were the men whom we invited to speak at our meetings and to contribute articles to our magazine *The Student World.* This was not always appreciated by the older generation nor by the authorities. When in 1939 Reinhold Niebuhr had been invited to speak at the World Christian Youth Conference in Amsterdam, the Netherlands government at first refused to issue him the necessary visa. I called on the Minister of Foreign Affairs and was told that Niebuhr was known to speak favourably of communism. I replied that Niebuhr was a socialist, and very critical of communism. The minister, although he finally granted the visa, was of the opinion that socialists and communists were much the same thing. He had clearly not yet discovered how the world had changed, for a few weeks later, the first socialist ministers took their places in the Dutch cabinet.

Let us now consider what part the church has played in the development of social thought. I have already spoken of the patriarchal element in the traditional teaching of the church. It is remarkable that, in this respect, there was no break with the past at the Reformation. Thomas Aquinas had taught that the family was the basic unit of society and that social ethics should therefore be conceived as the application of the commandments relating to family life in other spheres of society. Roman Catholic thinking continued along these lines, considering that society must necessarily be organized in a hierarchical and patriarchal manner. This view of human relations in the social order has been described as 'familiarism'.[1]

The word 'familiarism' can however equally well be used for the social ethics of Luther and Calvin. This is particularly clear in Luther's *Great Catechism*. In his explanation of the commandment to honour one's parents, he lists three types of 'father': "of the blood, of the house, of the country". The 'house' was the extended family which was the chief economic unit in society. Parents had authority over their children and "from this authority proceeds and spreads out all the rest". He continues: "That is why men-servants and maid-servants must not only obey their masters and mistresses, but must also respect them as they would their own fathers and mothers and fulfil all the duties expected of them."

Calvin also insisted that there was a hierarchy in society which had to be respected. There were those called to command and those called to obey. To servants he said: "It is God who has put this burden on your shoulders, that your work and industry is hired by your masters."[2] He points out that we all have one and the same Father in Heaven, "but that does not change the fact that some are given a low place and others a higher place, and that we must accept our station without demur." Calvin applied the commandment to honour parents also to all other relationships which are of a hierarchical nature, saying: "Thus the Lord gives us without doubt a universal rule — that to those whom we recognize as having been ordained our superiors we give our respect, our reverence and our love."[3]

Through catechisms, sermons and religious literature this conception of the relations between master and servant for long dominated European thinking about life. It was the ideal of a coherent, ordered and graded society in which each class performed its specific function and in which all had duties towards the other classes. The severity of the subordination of the servant class was mitigated, for masters were obliged to treat their servants with paternal care. In all churches, teachers and preachers warned in strong terms against exploitation of servants or refusal to pay just wages.

At the same time, the strong emphasis laid upon the ultimate equality of all children of the heavenly Father contained a dynamic element which might have revolutionary consequences. This element was not yet apparent in Luther's thought. He was anxious to maintain the spiritual purity of the gospel and therefore reacted strongly against social revolutionaries who interpreted spiritual equality in economic or political terms. When peasants in Swabia and Franconia rose in revolt and fought the Peasants' War (1524-25) Luther repudiated them. Replying to their revolutionary Twelve Articles, he wrote: "This article would make all men equal and so change the spiritual kingdom of Christ into an external worldly one. Impossible! An earthly kingdom cannot exist without inequality of persons. Some must be free, others serfs, some rulers, others subjects. As St Paul says: 'Before Christ both master and slave are one.' "[4]

Calvin has a more dynamic conception of the role of Christians in society. He wrote that God has created the world in order that it might become the theatre of his glory. Christians were called upon to participate in God's plan, which consisted in the restoration of the social order through resistance to its sinful aspects. Thus Calvin feared the social implications of the spiritual equality less than Luther. He even went so far as to suggest that the claim of the poor for justice, with its source and norm in belief in equality, would finally be granted by God.[5]

Calvin thus tried to affirm two apparently contradictory theories: first, that Christians had to accept as divinely ordained the differences in status, and the subordination of some to others apparent in the society in which they lived, and second, that Christians had to participate in a process through which the worst consequences of those inequalities would be corrected. Property was not a private matter. It was a gift of God to be used in the service of people. "Abstenance from evil actions is not enough to satisfy God, who has given men mutual obligations so that they might profit from and help one another. That is why we are told to be generous and to fulfil all duties through which the fellowship *(com-*

pagnie) and community of men are maintained. Thus, in order not to be condemned by God as thieves, we must ensure as far as possible that everyone can keep his property in safety and use it for the benefit of his brethren, just as we should do ourselves."[6]

As long as the family was the principal economic unit and while economic and social relationships were mainly of a personal nature, the conception of society as an integrated patriarchal family was valid. In the seventeenth century, however, new economic forces overcame many traditional forms and created a society which had very little resemblance to a family and in which family ethics became increasingly irrelevant. R. H. Tawney made this point with force: "Faced with the problem of a wage-earning proletariat, it (religious teaching) could do no more than repeat with meaningless iteration its traditional lore as to the duties of master to servant and servant to master. It had insisted that all men were brethren. But it did not occur to it to point out that, as a result of the new economic imperialism, which was beginning to develop in the seventeenth century, the brethren of the English merchant were the Africans whom he kidnapped for slavery in America, or the American Indians whom he stripped of their lands, or the Indian craftsmen from whom he bought muslins and silks at starvation prices."[7]

A frontal attack on the idea of society as a family was made by John Locke. In his debate with Sir Robert Filmer on the nature of government, he pointed out that the power of a magistrate over the people, the power of a master over his servants and the power of a father over his children were different in nature. Masters had only temporary power over servants "and no greater than what is contained in the contract between them." Even parents had only temporary authority over their children, for the commandment did not say that children were to obey their parents once they had grown up, though they should continue to honour them. As a successor to a society modelled on the family, Locke proposed bluntly: "The great and chief end therefore, of Men's uniting into Commonwealths, and putting themselves under Government, is the preservation of their Property."[8]

This demolition of the traditional patriarchal order of society indeed implied an emancipation, but for whom? Was it for men of property, for the masters and not for the servants? Did it mean that those who were considered as full members of society had no longer to concern themselves about the traditional rules and obligations?

The inevitable result was that the 'have-nots' became outsiders. The emancipation of the masters meant that the servants were less emancipated than ever. Auguste Comte described them later as people who did not belong to the nation, but camped on its territory like foreign nomads. The masters believed it to be true, in theory and practice, that servants would not work more, but rather less, if their wages were increased. In 1771, Arthur Young wrote: "Everyone but an idiot knows that the lower classes must be kept poor, or they will never be industrious."[9]

The churches continued to preach the traditional social ethic and did not realize that their message was becoming increasingly irrelevant. When, in one of his famous sermons, Bossuet said of the ruling class: "God has made them great so that they may serve as fathers to his poor people", the powerful men in his congregation must have been flattered, but the poor must have wondered why they saw no sign of this paternal care.

Society thus continued to be careless of the poor, oppressed or underprivileged among its members. Even the slave trade met with little criticism and was seen as part of an economic process which obeyed its own laws. Slaves were by nature servants and should remain under the control of their masters. It was the issue of the slave trade, however, which finally produced a moral reaction. More and more men and women began to see that there were limits to economic freedom and to believe that no one had the right to treat other human beings as if they were cattle. The Quakers were among the first to protest. Later, Wilberforce, who fought the slave trade for twenty years until it was at last abolished, presented his case as a clear choice between God and Mammon. To say that the slave trade had to be maintained because it was in the national interest was "but to dethrone the moral Governor of the universe, and to fall down and worship the idol of interest." Yet it took many years of struggle after the slave trade had been stopped to achieve the abolition of slavery itself, and when emancipation came, it was by no means a day of pure joy for the slaves. In his autobiography, *Up from Slavery*, the great American black leader, Booker T. Washington, described his feelings and those of other slaves when they were told that they were free people. Then, he continued: "The wild rejoicing on the part of the emancipated coloured people lasted but for a brief period... The great responsibility of being free, of having charge of themselves and their children, seemed to take possession of them... Was it any wonder that within a few hours the wild rejoicing ceased and a feeling of deep gloom seemed to pervade the slave quarters?"[10] This reaction, athough it must have seemed strange at the time, was a natural one, as the weight of responsibility for their own lives fell on the former slaves, a necessary stage on the road towards a fuller emancipation.

The situation of the lower classes had thus become decidedly worse and it is remarkable that they remained passive for so long. Here and there there were risings of a revolutionary nature against the prevailing social structure, but these led nowhere and their leaders had no clear programme. The major revolutionary movements of the eighteenth and the first half of the nineteenth centuries had objectives other than the greater wellbeing of the working classes. The American Revolution was a struggle for independence from the mother country, led by an emancipated bourgeoisie, which had no intention of applying the principles of the Declaration of Rights to the sphere of social or economic relations. In the French Revolution, the small group of radicals who wished to introduce a regime of social equality was treated as dangerous conspirators and its leader, Grachus Baboeuf, was condemned to death. The risings in the revolutionary year of 1848 were of a nationalist rather than a social nature, risings against despotism and foreign rule rather than against social inequality, and, gallant though many of them were, they failed to transform anything.

It was in 1848 that the Communist Manifesto of Marx and Engels appeared, too late to influence the events of that year in any way.

In the second half of the nineteenth century, however, the emancipation of the workers was no longer a dream but the concrete objective of a well-organized movement with a clear programme. Even more important, it had an inspiring conception of a new society in which the disinherited would at last reach their proper place. It has often been said that Marx was, before all, the prophet of a new religion. Schumpeter, the Austrian economist, for example, maintained that the greatness of Marx's achievement was that to millions of human hearts his promise of a terrestrial paradise to be achieved through socialism gave a new meaning to life.[11] The Dutch poet, Henriette Roland Holst, for many years an active leader of the Communist Party, described Marx's voice as "heavy as a trombone, the prophetic tone from the old garden of Israel... the pulse of the lords beats wildly in anger or faintly in fear, the pulse of the servants becomes strong and slow..."[12] She went on: "A great poem it was to see, in the shabby quarters of cities, long subservience transformed into noble pride, in men's eyes the fire of conscious dignity and in women's, so long reproachful like those of overdriven animals, the gleam of light and the soaring of hope and joy."[13] In other words, the socialist movement gave the dispossessed at last the possibility of belonging to a community with a great and glorious destiny. It was this, Marx's vision of the inclusion of the excluded rather than his economic theory, which gave Marxism its tremendous force.

In this way, Marx rediscovered the truth which had been obvious to medieval people and to the Reformers, that society needed a doctrine of cohesion, which could give all its members a sense of participation and responsibility. Marx could therefore speak with appreciation, almost with nostalgia, of the traditional patriarchal society. He stated in the Communist Manifesto: "The bourgeoisie, wherever it got the upper hand, put an end to all feudal, patriarchal, idyllic relations, pitilessly tore asunder the motley feudal ties that bound man to his natural superiors and left remaining no other bond between man and man than naked self-interest and callous cash payment."

It is therefore not astonishing that there is a strong resemblance between Calvin and Marx with regard to the ultimate goal towards which society should move. Calvin, in his commentary on the Second Epistle of St Paul to the Corinthians (8:13), wrote: "Thus God wills that there shall be such an analogy and equality among us that everyone helps the poor according to his ability in order that some may not have superfluous goods and others suffer from want." Karl Marx, and later also Lenin, quoted with approval the formula of Louis Blanc: "From each according to his ability, to each according to his needs." It is unlikely that Marx had read Calvin's commentaries but he shared with him the desire for a society in which there would be total solidarity among people.

In his younger days, Marx defined emancipation as the application of the principle that "man is, for man, the supreme being". When servants were truly emancipated, when they were no longer forced to live as obedient sons of their masters, they could at last live as brothers. Religion could be abolished because it was no more than a consolation for people who needed it in their misery, and was entirely superfluous when that misery had been overcome. "Religion is merely the illusory sun which moves around man as long as he does not move around himself."[14] Marx continued: "The critique of religion leads to the categorical imperative to overthrow all social conditions in which man is a humiliated, subservient, abandoned, despicable being." In his view, the proletariat must now become the central figure in society, because they represented the only class that had not exploited others. This, he believed, would inaugurate the era of true freedom and solidarity.

How was this to be done? To this question Marx did not give a sufficiently clear answer. The men and women of the Third International, following Lenin, emphasized that the Communist Manifesto had called for revolutionary action and had proclaimed the necessity of the dictatorship of the proletariat. This dictatorship was to be a stage on the road to a fully Communist society. In fact, it proved to be a lasting characteristic of Communist societies.

As Communist dictatorships in existence today are exercised by strongly centralized Communist parties with powerful executive committees, the question arises whether paternalism has really been overcome, or whether the 'little father' who ruled as Czar has not simply been replaced by one or more 'little fathers' in the Kremlin, or in other Communist strongholds.

In his book *Authority,* published in 1980, Richard Sennett remarks: "Paternalism is something more than a passing phase in the history of capitalism. It has passed into the language of revolutionary socialism. From the 1920s on Soviet Russian leaders began to make use of it, and the usage has been repeated in more recent socialist regimes." Stalin's saying — "The state is a family, and I am your father" — is a forceful example of this. Karl Marx, in whose thought the total emancipation of the human being was a central conception, would hardly have approved of such language. Was he not himself, however, responsible for this neo-paternalism? When he proclaimed the need for the dictatorship of the proletariat, he had taken back with one hand what he had given with the other, and he became, as Peter Berglar put it, "a dreamer who is unconsciously imprisoned in the world of the fathers".[15]

The contrast between the promise which Marxism seemed to offer and the reality as it appeared when certain countries adopted Communist regimes created a deep crisis in the ranks of those with Socialist sympathies. In 1931, Nicolas Berdyaev gave me for publication in *The Student World* a deeply penetrating article. Berdyaev, who had been a Marxist but had been forced to leave the Soviet Union because of his strong defence of freedom of conscience, wrote: "The most important thing is freedom for the human soul. It is impossible to organize a perfect society by force and to abolish evil by external and mechanical means." Henriette Roland Holst who, as I have said, had been an enthusiastic activist in the ranks of the Communist Party, described her very deep disillusionment in her later poems. "Is this socialism?" she wrote. "Its face does not express the old glorious dream, it does not radiate light, nor freedom nor beauty. What is left of you, Socialism, my beloved?" One of her last poems reads: "Brotherhood is not able to bind hearts together, unless these hearts rediscover a Father, bow down humbly before his high authority and, loving one another in Him, rejoice...."[16]

Other Marxists, together with British socialists whose socialism sprang from other roots, believed in a gradual progress towards the new society, to be achieved by democratic means. They succeeded in a remarkably short time in making for the trade union movement and for socialist or labour parties a decisively important place in the economic and political field.

Had the problem of the relationship between masters and servants now been solved? In one way it had, for there were no longer patient, poor and lowly servants who meekly obeyed their masters. Men and women in all stations of life had become conscious of their dignity as human beings. But were they emancipated in the sense of being masters of their own fate? The great majority were still dependent on forces over which they had little or no control. If they were no longer in the service of paternal masters, they were at the mercy of a complex economic process in which the masters could no longer be identified, because even those in leading positions were only managers acting on behalf of anonymous forces.

At the time when the Industrial Revolution and the rise of the socialist movement produced many acute social problems, the churches failed to give any constructive moral guidance. The Roman Catholic Church, it is true, spoke up, but mainly by issuing warnings against socialism. A more positive message was contained in the Encyclical *Rerum Novarum* issued in 1891, which proved to be the point of departure for much social activity, but its concept of society was based largely on traditional family ethics which were not applicable to the complexities of the modern economic system.

Similarly, the first ecumenical conference of the churches, convened by Archbishop Nathan Söderblom at Stockholm in 1925, had as its theme 'Life and Work' and expressed the conviction that Christian principles must be applied to the life of society. The conference did not, however, tackle the basic issue of the structure of the economic order. I attended that conference as the youngest and most inexperienced of all the delegates, and was impressed by the vigour of the 'social gospel', the doctrine propagated by the large American delegation concerning the relevance of Christianity to social life. I later made a special study of that doctrine in a doctor's thesis entitled *The Background of the Social Gospel in America (1928)*. I came to the conclusion that here too the family served as the prototype of social organization and that the ethics preached by followers of the social gospel were essentially the application of family ethics to a wider world. Soon afterwards, Reinhold Niebuhr demanded whether the ethical principles governing personal relations in the family could have any relevance in the impersonal world of large corporations, bureaucracies and anonymous financial power. Similarly, Dr J. H. Oldham, while preparing for the second conference on 'Life and Work', to be held in Oxford in 1937, said: "It is only too evident that man has become enslaved by forces which his own purposes had brought into existence... A company may do things in the interest of shareholders which its directors might hesitate to do as individuals, as it may refrain, and ought often to refrain, from doing things which individuals are free to do."[17] The Oxford conference, in which a considerable number of laymen participated, dealt not only with the spirit which ought to permeate social relationships but also looked critically at the structure of modern society. The next step was taken at the first Assembly of the World Council of Churches,

at Amsterdam in 1948, which accepted a proposal made by Dr
Oldham to use the concept of 'the responsible society' as the criterion by which we should judge all existing social and economic
systems and as a standard to guide us in the specific choices we
must make.

The concept of 'the responsible society' has three dimensions. It
deals first with the responsibility of the whole of society for all its
members, especially for its weakest and poorest members. It
should be an obvious truth, which unfortunately has not yet
become generally accepted, that in this modern, interdependent
world, it is not a question of charity, but of justice, to ensure that
underprivileged people and nations receive the help necessary to
enable them to overcome the problems of poverty and famine. In
the second place, a responsible society is one in which all members
who have come of age can participate as responsible citizens in the
making of decisions on the social and economic developments
which affect their lives. Addressing the World Conference on
Church and Society held in Geneva in 1966, I said: "We have now
learned that there are different ways of depriving men of the possibility of acting responsibly. There is not only the way of autocracy and dictatorship, there is also the much more subtle way of
giving man the impression that every important question is
decided for him." In a truly responsible society, it should no
longer be possible that workers who have given the best years of
their lives to a particular enterprise or company are dismissed
without previous consultation, become unemployed, and are thus
in reality treated as if they were merely servants, and servants of
masters who have no paternal conscience. A responsible society
would also find ways and means of preventing vast multinational
companies, some of them with hundreds of thousands of
employees in up to one hundred countries, from being a law unto
themselves, but would render them clearly accountable not only to
their shareholders but also to representative organs of their
employees and clients.

A responsible society is, in the third place, one which recognizes
that it is not an end in itself, but that it must serve a higher aim.
Religious people would call this the responsibility of society to
God, but all should be able to agree that the human person is not
merely a social being, and that the socio-economic order must
therefore never make a total claim on the human being. If emanci-

pation means the opportunity of living and acting as a fully responsible human being, the freeing of servants from the paternalism of masters proves to be not the final, but only the first stage in a long process towards full social liberty.

6. Emancipation from colonial paternalism

In the history of the Western domination of Asia, Africa and Latin America, we find the West represented at different times by four different types of people — the missionary, the trader, the empire-builder and the guardian. It started with the missionaries. In 1454, Pope Nicholas V gave to the Portuguese "the right, total and absolute, to invade, conquer and subject all the countries which are under the rule of the enemies of Christ, Saracen or Pagan" with the objective of "giving them knowledge of the name of Christ". In 1494, when a treaty was concluded between Portugal and Spain, according to which they divided the world outside Europe between them, that purpose remained unchanged. It was, as has often been remarked, a continuation of the Crusades.

The pre-eminent nature of this missionary task was however soon forgotten. After the sixteenth century, the time of Bartolomé de las Casas and St Francis Xavier, missions were overshadowed by trading posts and commercial exploitation. Already in 1535 Erasmus had written: "There is all the difference in the world between robbery and Christian warfare, between preaching the Kingdom of Faith and setting up tyrants with their interest in this world, between seeking the safety of souls and pursuing the spoils of Mammon."[1]

It was characteristic of the era of traders that the people of the recently discovered continents were considered to be of no importance. The directors of the Dutch East India Company opposed the use of their ships to bring food to areas where severe famine raged, because the vessels were intended to serve the interests of the company and were not to be used for the "feeding of people, with whom we have, properly speaking, nothing to do." Such a complete rejection of responsibility for people with whom they were in daily contact and whose services they enjoyed can only be explained, though not justified, by the fact that the Europeans did not consider them as fully human. It was for this reason too that the unspeakably horrible slave trade of modern history became possible. The slave traders were completely blind to the fact that the slaves were human beings, and could not conceive that these men and women had feelings similar to their own. Solemn declarations were adopted concerning the rights of men, but it occurred only to a small group of Evangelicals, Quakers and other idealists to raise the issue of the compatibility of human rights with slavery.

The period of the traders was long. The Dutch East India Company, for which political interests were always subordinated to those of commerce, went out of existence in 1807, to be replaced by the rule of a Governor General appointed by the Netherlands. The British East India Company, whose merchants, as Jawaharlal Nehru put it, "were interested in dividends and treasure and not in the improvement or even protection of those who had come under their sway",[2] survived until 1874, although the task of governing India had been transferred by act of parliament to the crown in 1858.

In the second half of the nineteenth century, therefore, it was the empire-builders who came to the fore. Trade was no longer the only consideration in the attitude of the rulers to the dependent peoples. There was also the great task of ruling over huge masses of people, demonstrating the remarkable European genius for organization and legislation, of introducing into this wider world all the latest results of modern science and technology.

The colonists now showed a clear sense of responsibility for the colonized, but their attitude remained very largely that of the master to the servant. It 1883, Seton Kerr, who had been Foreign Secretary in the government of India, spoke of "the cherished conviction which was shared by every Englishman in India, from the highest to the lowest, by the planter's assistant in his lowly bungalow and by the editor in the full light of the presidency town — from those to the Chief Commissioner in charge of the important province and to the Viceroy on his throne — the conviction that he belongs to a race whom God has destined to govern and subdue."[3]

In the last decades of the nineteenth century and the first years of the twentieth, there was in the West a general imperialist fever. "The colonial microbe", said Lord Rosebery, "has penetrated almost every empire." The scramble for Africa involved the British, French, Germans, Italians and Belgians, while the Russians, Japanese and Dutch, and even the Americans who had anti-colonialism in their blood, sought to extend their territory. *The Washington Post* wrote in 1898: "We are animated by a new sensation... The taste of Empire is in the mouth of the people even as the taste of blood in the jungle."

The French talked of their *mission civilisatrice* and the Germans about their *Kultur,* which should be brought to other parts of the world. The Russian and American expansion, although it took place over their own continents, and not overseas, was still colonization, dominating the original inhabitants.

The empire-builders did not remain unchallenged, however. There were many in Western countries who felt uneasy about an imperialism which seemed to be pure power politics. If the nineteenth century, as Lord Rosebery said, was 'an era of emancipation', how could the colonial powers justify the extension of their rule over peoples who had so far been independent? The *humanitaires* in France pointed out the contrast between their government's conquests and the republican tradition of the rights of people. "We are preparing to celebrate 1789 and we tyrannize the weak," exclaimed a prominent French naval officer.[4] During the debate on colonial expansion in the United States of America, a number of the foremost intellectual leaders, like William James, the psychologist and philosopher, and President Charles William Eliot of Harvard, spoke out strongly against 'jingoism', as aggressive patriotism had come to be called. They agreed with the historian, James Bryce, that "to yield to the earth-hunger now raging among the European states would be a complete departure from the maxims of the illustrious founders of the republic."[5]

It was while this sharp controversy on colonial expansion was raging in the United States that Rudyard Kipling's poem "The White Man's Burden" appeared. It was addressed to the Americans and was very widely reprinted and quoted, "doing much to reconcile the hesitant to the imperial task."[6] Kipling's conception of colonialism seemed to make imperialism morally respectable:

Take up the White Man's burden
    Send forth the best ye breed.
Go bind your sons to exile
    To serve your captives' need;
To wait in heavy harness
    On fluttered folk and wild
Your new caught sullen peoples
    Half devil and half child...

By open speech and simple
    And hundred times made plain,
To seek another's profit
    And work another's gain...
Take up the White Man's burden
    And reap his old reward:
The blame of those ye better
    The hate of those ye guard.

In Kipling's opinion, therefore, there was nothing objectionable about an empire-builder as long as he was at the same time a guardian seeking the profit of his ward. The representative of the colonial power was to be a teacher whose task was to guide, instruct and protect the colonized people until they had come of age and could be emancipated. In Christian circles, this guardianship was conceived as a divine calling. Thus, in his "Ode to the Nineteenth Century", Francis Thompson has these lines:

Thou, spacious Century!
    Hast seen the Western knee
Set on the Asian neck,
    The dusty Africa
Kneel to imperial Europe's beck;
    The West for her permitted while didst see
Stand mistress-wise and tutelar
    To the grey nations dreaming on their days afar
From old forgotten war
    Folding hands whence has slid disused rule;
The while, unprescient, in her regent school
    She shapes the ample days and things to be,
And large new empery.

In more prosaic terms, that was to say that the colonial world was essentially a school in which the natives were children under the tutelage of their Western rulers.

This conception was elaborated by Abraham Kuyper, the leader of the Anti-Revolutionary Party in the Netherlands, who was prime minister from 1901 to 1905. In *Our Programme*, he stated that the system of guardianship in the colonies was clearly the only one that could be defended from a Christian point of view. Guardianship meant treating the colonial peoples as not yet grown up and therefore accepting the threefold obligation which all guardians had to their wards, to give them moral education, to administer their goods with care and to enable them, in the future, if it were God's will, to adopt a more independent position.

When guardianship and preparation for emancipation became the main arguments in favour of the colonial relationship, the dependent peoples began to ask whether there was clear evidence that they were being helped to advance on the road to self-government, and whether the European paternalists really wanted their pupils to grow up. The first answer to these questions was seen to be the great progress being made in the realm of education, in which field the missionaries had played a pioneering role. In India, at the beginning of the nineteenth century, William Carey and his associates had established a number of schools in Bengal. In 1855, Macaulay convinced the British authorities that English should be the teaching language in the schools, and soon after that, the first universities in India were founded.

The French and the Dutch, in fact all colonial powers, also introduced their languages as the medium of teaching in their territories. As these languages were also the official languages used in the areas concerned, pupils were prepared for clerical and other jobs, and provided access to the culture of their rulers.

The results of this spread of education, however, were not quite what the governments had expected. It has been thought that as Asian or African students came to know the history, philosophy and literature of their guardians, they would become deeply attached to the culture of these European countries. Although, of course, many did develop a love for these things, dangerous questions also began to be asked. Students in the Netherlands East Indies learned how William the Silent had fought for the liberation of his country, and heard the Dutch national anthem celebrating the abolition of tyranny. Their thoughts then turned, not to sixteenth century Spain, but to the Dutch power now in their own land. In French colonies, students learned of the rights of man, and wondered whether the Marseillaise was not applicable to their own situation. In British territories, they heard of the Glorious Revolution of 1689. They heard how Byron had died fighting for the independence of Greece, and must have asked themselves whether an English poet should not come to fight for their freedom.

The introduction of Western culture to Eastern or African peoples thus led to great disappointment. Rabindranath Tagore said at the very end of his life that as he got to know English thought and literature, he had set the English on the throne of his heart. He had believed that the victor would of his own grace pave the way of freedom for the vanquished, but there had come a parting of the ways and he had become disillusioned as he increasingly discovered how easily those who accepted the highest truths of civilization disowned them with impunity whenever questions of their national self-interest were involved.[7]

At the end of the nineteenth and the beginning of the twentieth century, the pupils began to take things into their own hands. The time of docile waiting for real emancipation was over. National movements were created and developed with remarkable speed. Three wars gave powerful support to the cause of nationalism. The first was the Russo-Japanese War of 1904 in which, for the first time in living memory, an Asian power had defeated a European one. C. F. Andrews, the friend of Gandhi and Tagore, wrote that, as a result of this victory by Japan, "Asia was moved from one end to the other and the sleep of centuries was finally broken... The old time glory and greatness of Asia seemed destined to return... Behind these dreams and visions was the one exalting hope — that the days of servitude to the West were over and the day of independence had dawned."[8] The First World War produced a further 'de-glorification of the West' and the Second proved to be the last shock which hastened the collapse of the whole colonial system established by Western Europe.

Who could have foreseen that the rise of nationalism in Asia and Africa would be such an explosive process and that the period until emancipation would be so short? The guardians had certainly not expected this, but had believed that they could count on a very long period of rule. John Morley, Secretary of State for India, said in the early years of the twentieth century that he could not conceive of democratic institutions in India even in the far distant future.[9] Lord Curzon, Viceroy of India at the time of the great Durbar of 1903, refused to allow the singing of the hymn "Onward Christian Soldiers", not because of its opening words, but because it contained the lines "Crowns and thrones may perish, Kingdoms rise and wane". He did not consider that this was the note to be sounded when celebrating the glory of the British Empire. B. C. de Jonge, Governor General of the Netherlands East Indies, said in the 1930s to the nationalist leaders there that the Dutch had been in the Indies for 300 years, and it would surely take another 300 before the territory would be ready for independence.

The inability of many rulers to take emancipation seriously and their unchanging style of paternalistic domination led to a deep rupture between the Europeans and the Asians and Africans. When I visited Asia in 1933 and 1934, I was made vividly aware of this tragic development. My wife's uncle was at that time Governor General of the Netherlands East Indies, so that we spent some time at the palace at Buitenzorg, where we lived in the patriarchal atmosphere surrounding the *Landvoogd,* or Guardian of the Land, as was his title. We spent more time, however, with the Indonesian students and those of other Asian countries who had come to Java to participate in the first Asia conference of the World Student Christian Federation. The contrast between the official Dutch world and that of the Asian students was enormous. The Governor General maintained that all talk about independence, even independence in the future, was in fact undermining the authority of the government. He was a paternalistic ruler with a deep sense of responsibility, devoted to his task, and willing to give help when needed. He had also, however, the strong conviction that Dutch rule was right. He insisted on strict discipline and reacted immediately against any attempt to propagate the loosening or breaking of the country's ties with the Netherlands. In that other world, however, the world of the students, there was general agreement that all colonial domination should come to an end in the very near future. The chairman of the young Student Christian Movement of Java, Dr Johannes Leimena, told us that the national movement was progressing, that no article of law could stop it and that it was the duty of Christians to participate in it. We did not realize at that time that we were listening to the future Deputy Prime Minister of the Republic of Indonesia. At the conference, the Asian students were unanimous in rejecting

Western domination. They would no longer accept, as the report on the conference stated, that "the East must cooperate, but the West shall direct. We may say this to the West: the East has become so sensitive that this relation is regarded as sinister. It must be revised. Ours should be the initiation and control, while we welcome the cooperation of the West."[10]

A few weeks later, I found an even sharper situation of conflict in India. I visited Pandit Nehru in his family home in Allahabad. He had just come out of prison and was preparing for the next round in the struggle with the government of India. He accepted my invitation to address the large conference which the Indian Student Christian Movement was holding in the city and received a tremendous response. This 'idol of young India', as he was called, did not accept worship, but gave the students a meaningful task as he called on them to serve the great cause of freedom.

These were my experiences in 1934. In 1939 came the Second World War, during which the French and Dutch colonial territories in Asia, together with large parts of the British Empire there, were suddenly conquered by Japan. The myth of the invincibility of the Western powers had been disproved. The government of Japan, itself an example of supreme patriarchal rule — the Emperor was even a god — encouraged nationalist movements, but hoped to keep the 'co-prosperity sphere' under its domination. The Western powers retaliated by adopting the Atlantic Charter. This seemed to open the way towards full emancipation, for it declared that states would "respect the right of every people to choose its own form of government." Once again there came disappointment, for in various ways it was made clear, as *The Economist* put it in 1945, that "none of them (the colonial powers) has any intention of abandoning its colonial empire."[11]

However, the forces working for emancipation had now gathered so much momentum that it was impossible to stop them. Following the appointment of Earl Mountbatten of Burma as Viceroy of India, that sub-continent, in 1947, achieved independence, as the two sovereign states of India and Pakistan. The Netherlands East Indies became the independent Republic of Indonesia in 1949.

My experiences in Asia that year were very different from those of 1934. In the palace in Batavia, soon to be renamed Jakarta, where our uncle had lived in splendid style as Governor General, I found the last representatives of the Dutch government, in no cheerful mood, preparing to leave, while in the city of Jogjakarta were President Soekarno and the first government of the Republic of Indonesia, full of enthusiasm for the future. In India, Pandit Nehru, no longer a regular inmate of prisons, lived in the Prime Minister's residence. I found him the same sober and realistic leader who knew that emancipation from foreign domination was not, important though it was, the beginning of the millenium.

So, throughout the 1950s and the decades that followed, the process of emancipation spread to other countries in Asia, to Africa and to other parts of the world. In some cases, the colonial powers had felt 'the winds of change' and had prepared for their departure by training cadres to assume responsibility, not only for the government of the young state, but also for its civil service, police and other necessary functions. Other masters resisted the inevitable so that some countries won their independence in the blood and tears of war.

I witnessed the final acts of some of the colonial dramas, and the first acts of some in the era of freedom. There was in all these the same strange mixture of euphoria and anxiety for the future which Booker T. Washington had described as a feature of the emancipation of the slaves. Perhaps in the new young states, this reaction was not so extreme, but it was soon realized that political emancipation did not mean economic emancipation. The rich nations, not all of them former colonial powers, would continue to use the existing economic system for their own benefit. Emancipation would also be incomplete as long as corruption, exploitation and greed undermined the national life, in short, until the emancipated nations learned to discipline themselves.

While these tremendous changes were taking place in many parts of the world, there was one country where the relations between the dominant minority and the controlled majority remained unchanged. This was, of course, South Africa. For the whole period of my acquaintance with that country, some thirty years, relations between whites and blacks have been characterized by an astonishing immobility. It is not that there had been any lack of plans for solving the national problem, but these plans had not been carried out, or had been totally ineffective. For example, although the government of South Africa created Bantustans, no objective student of the South African scene can take this seriously as an answer to the fundamental questions of South African society.

The idea of guardianship has played a very important role in South Africa. It is not *apartheid* alone, but *apartheid* together with guardianship which is the basis of the Afrikaner ideology. *Apartheid* alone, if interpreted as "development according to kind", could be applied in a manner acceptable to all concerned. Guardianship, as we have seen, can be a constructive motive. But when *apartheid* and guardianship are combined, the result is disastrous, for then the ruling minority says: "I am your guardian. I alone decide how and when and where your specific development shall take place. You must be patient and grateful, and not speak unless you are asked to do so."

The defenders of the official ideology do not deny the right of the black, coloured and Indian people to freedom and participation. One of the reports of a church congress held in Bloemfontein in 1950, where a very comprehensive interpretation of Afrikaner ideology and theology was given, stated clearly: "No people in the world worth their salt will be content indefinitely with no say, or only an indirect say, in the affairs of the state or in the socio-economic organization of the country in which decisions are taken about their interests and future."[12] This seemed a good basis for a true dialogue between the races. This dialogue did not take place however for, as was said elsewhere in the report, the non-whites as minors are entrusted to the whites who are their guardians, and the guardians know whether it is time to take further steps towards emancipation or not. In fact, guardianship has now become the justification for immobility. The warning given by Professor Ben Marais, in *Ekumene onder die Suiderkruis* published in 1979, that guardianship was a temporary and not a permanent relationship, was ignored.

I had the opportunity to get to know some of the leaders of the black South Africans and was deeply impressed by their attitude. They were determined to fight for the rights of their people, but there was in them no bitterness or hatred. Leaders like Albert Luthuli, who received the Nobel Peace Prize, and Z. K. Matthews, who joined the World Council of Churches staff and later became Ambassador of Botswana in Washington, were ready for constructive cooperation between the races. And they were clearly in favour of using non-violent means to achieve the liberation of their people. In 1952, I spent some unforgettable hours in the settlement near Durban where Mahatma Gandhi had lived and where his son Manilal had become the director. Albert Luthuli was present. These two men, Gandhi and Luthuli, discussed with passionate intensity just how non-violent action could be applied to the racial situation in South Africa. One saw the possibility of a peaceful solution of South Africa's fundamental problem. But would the white man climb down from his pedestal and be willing to listen to his black neighbour? And if not, what could these wise men say to the younger generation?

In 1960, after the Sharpeville disturbances, the World Council of Churches tried to encourage the South African churches to overcome the impasse in the racial situation. Their efforts at first met with remarkable success but later struck the determined opposition of the political party in power. Perhaps the only real achievement was the creation of the Christian Institute which, under the courageous leadership of Beiers Naudé, has been pioneering in the search for a constructive solution. South Africa has thus made no real progress in emancipation during the very decades in which relations between dependent peoples and their ruling guardians have changed profoundly.

At the end of the Second World War, at the very time when the emancipation of overseas colonies was beginning to come about, new cases occurred of the subjection of whole nations to the domination of foreign governments. The USSR acted in a number of countries just as the imperial power had done in the colonial era. This domination continues and is even being extended to new areas. There is however a distinction, though without a difference, in the words used to justify these acts. Lenin had said: "All my life and strength were given to the first cause in the world — the liberation of mankind." His successors have chosen to interpret this as giving them the right and duty to liberate peoples against their will and in ways which they had not chosen, making of such emancipation a tragedy, which will certainly have repercussions on the future of the world.

7. Women seek emancipation from male paternalism

It must have been in 1910 or 1911. On my way to school, I saw a lady trying to sell leaflets in the street, calling out in a monotonous voice: "Women must remain women — two cents." That was my first impression of the great battle about women's rights, fought particularly fiercely by Britain's suffragettes, but also raging in the Netherlands. Young as I was, I did not see why I should pay two cents to be told the obvious truth that women should remain women.

For a long time I was puzzled by the necessity of discussion about the place of women in society. In our family, the strongest personalities were women. When I went to university, however, I became part of a self-conscious masculine world. Women students were still a recent phenomenon. They were tolerated but did not share fully in the life of the university. For example, they were not accepted as members of most of the traditional student clubs and societies. At a lecture given by a famous professor of philosophy attended by a few women students, I heard him exclaim: "There they sit in the School of Pure Reason... while they ought rather to be producing children." It did not occur to this fervent Hegelian that women might discover a dialectic relationship between philosophy and motherhood.

It is true however that at this same period, the Student Christian Movement was providing a milieu in which women had the same opportunities as men to make their contribution.

It was through my wife that I became aware of the real issue. She had received the rather superficial education given to young ladies in the early decades of this century. It seemed to her unfair that the men in her family had, as a matter of course, received a university education, while the women got an education based on the idea that they should know a bit about everything, but nothing very thoroughly. This was for her a typical example of the masculine domination of society. As she began to study the question more deeply, she came to feel that the unequal treatment of women in the economic and political field to which feminists paid so much attention was only a symptom of a deeper malady. The real problem was a spiritual and religious one. In her first article on the subject, written in 1934, she said that women should stop adapting themselves to a man-made world, for by doing so they "only strengthened man's belief in the legitimate character of his monopoly of human norms and values and his deep-rooted conviction that he alone, without the woman, represents the true homo sapiens."[1] This was at the time a new and somewhat unexpected approach. In this article, and also in a letter written in the same year to Karl Barth, she raised the question as to whether St Paul's statement in the First Epistle to the Corinthians that "man was not created for woman, but woman for man" must really be accepted. How could that assertion be reconciled with other statements of his concerning the interdependence of men and women? "St Paul must have over-estimated the resistance of woman's nerves, if he thought she could stand the infernal isolation which must result from 'not being created for God' and 'man not being created for her'. All women felt a deep need, the need for an abiding, responsible authority, for one who takes her seriously, in fact for a Creator who had consciously made her a woman and who in doing so had a definite and profound purpose for the world." Barth answered her at length defending St Paul's conception of the superiority of man. St Paul had used this superiority as an illustration of the superiority of God over man, but the superiority of man over woman remained part of a God-given pattern of human life. My wife reacted with vigour, and made it clear that Barth had not convinced her. How could one compare the superiority of Christ over man with the superiority of man over woman?

She gave a fuller account of her increasingly strong convictions in a brochure published by the Dutch YWCA, under the title *Eve, Where Art Thou?*[2] In this publication, which was translated into English, French and German, she continued the discussion with Barth, telling how he had answered her criticism of the hierarchical conception of the relation between God-Christ-Man-Woman. Barth had written: "But don't you see that this puts a heavy burden on us men?" She had been deeply touched by this, but could not bring herself to believe that "God had given to one half of humanity a heavy burden on which to a large extent the salvation of the other half would depend." She felt therefore that women had done wrong in accepting the domination of men for they had in this way encouraged them in their self-complacency.

At first my wife felt rather alone in her search for a true spiritual emancipation of women, but after the Second World War she found many who shared her concern. I shall come back to the discussions of that period, but I must first make some remarks about earlier efforts to liberate women from male domination.

The history of the relations between the sexes is very largely a history of men's inhumanity to women. As more study is devoted to this subject, it appears increasingly astonishing that women have so long tolerated the treatment they received from their male partners. Among the many books which tell this story, Simone de Beauvoir's *Le deuxième sexe* is outstanding. It is more than a book, it is an impressive *J'accuse,* written with deep indignation. It is one-sided, it is often unfair, it is not always reliable, but someone had to write such a book to force men to take notice. Its thesis, that the history of women has been made by men and that women's problem has always been the problem of men's attitude to them, seems to me irrefutable. Whether Simone de Beauvoir draws the right conclusions from this fact is another question.

For a glance at the history of women's emancipation, the best point of departure is the French Revolution. Why so late, it may be asked. Did no woman, or for that matter no man, protest before that time against the autocratic rule of men? Indeed, there were individual voices. There were women who, without protesting, simply proved by their creative lives that it was nonsense to speak of the natural inferiority of their sex. It seems to me, however, that it was not until the last decades of the eighteenth century that we find the idea of women's emancipation stirring in a number of minds at once. The two principal centres of this movement were Paris and London. In October 1789, the women of Paris played a decisive role in the great revolution, when they marched to Versailles, demanded bread and forced the king and the queen to return with them to the capital city. It might then have been expected that the rights of man, which had just been proclaimed, would be interpreted as the rights of man *and woman,* and would thus establish their equality.

There were indeed people working towards this goal. Condorcet, the philosopher, who had already written on the subject, tried without success to change the constitution in this sense. In 1791, a courageous Frenchwoman, Olympe de Gouze, produced a *Déclaration des droits de la femme et de la citoyenne,* and women's clubs were founded in a number of places. The movement met with strong resistance, however. Olympe de Gouze was imprisoned, as was Théroigne de Mericourt, one of the leaders of the march to Versailles. Olympe de Gouze was condemned to death by the guillotine and died bravely.

During the same period, a considerable group of supporters of women's emancipation created a sensation in London. Mary Wollstonecraft was one of the first who succeeded in drawing attention to the cause of women. Her *A Vindication of the Rights of Woman* (1792) became a best-seller, according to her friend, later her husband, the anarchist philosopher Willaim Godwin. She had not minced her words, for she wrote: "Women may be convenient slaves but slavery will have its constant effect, degrading the master and the abject dependant."[3] The ideas discussed in the circle of Godwin's friends influenced the poet Shelley, who later married the daughter of Godwin and Mary Wollstonecraft. In his poem, "The Revolt of Islam" (1818), which is not about Islam, but as he stated in the preface, about "all the oppressions which are done under the sun", he asked: "Can man be free, if woman be a slave?" Later he wrote:

Woman, she is his slave, she has become
A thing I weep to speak, the child of scorn,
The outcast of a desolated home.

The first efforts towards the liberation of women remained, however, in the realm of Utopian dreams. The reality was more clearly to be seen in the Code Napoléon, which remained in force in certain countries during the whole of the nineteenth century. According to this Code, the *pater familias* was *seigneur et maître de la communauté,* to whom his wife owed obedience. Although for obvious historical reasons the Code Napoléon was never adopted in the United Kingdom, much time was to pass before women there were treated as equals before the law.

Strangely enough, little progress was made in the matter of women's rights in the early years of the nineteenth century. It was not until 1867 that John Stuart Mill, the foremost philosopher of his time, declared before the British parliament that the subordination of one sex to another was one of the main obstacles to human progress and that full equality between them should be established. Two years later appeared his *The Subjection of Women,* in which he wrote: "We have had the morality of submission, and the morality of chivalry and generosity; the time is now come for the morality of justice."

The first large-scale women's movement developed in the United States of America. It was the Women's Christian Temperance Union which organized a nation-wide crusade against alcoholic drinks and, in practice, for their prohibition. The leaders of this movement soon came to the conclusion, as one of them, Frances Willard, put it, that they needed the "woman's ballot as a weapon of protection to her home and to keep tempted loved ones from the tyranny of drink."[4] They therefore made common cause with the small group of women who were advocating votes for women. The link between the crusade against alcoholism and the fight for women's suffrage gave to the women's movement a 'moral fervour' of which it was in great need at a time when radical reformers were spreading the idea that supporters of suffrage for women intended to undermine family life and to preach free love.

The most famous suffragettes were, of course, those in the United Kingdom. They saw that the attempt to obtain the vote by persuasion was not producing adequate results and, in 1903, led by the distinguished figure of Mrs Pankhurst, they started a crusade in which extreme and violent means were used. Fights with the police, incendiarism, the slashing of paintings and physical attacks on politicians were among the methods which they employed to achieve their objective, the liberation of women from political impotence. H. G. Wells expressed the opinion that this "swarm of wildly exasperated human beings" was really an outburst against man's long arrogant assumption of superiority.[5]

It was not, however, until the First World War had shown how indispensable was the role of women at a time of crisis that any success crowned the suffragettes' efforts. It was not only in the United Kingdom that the First World War provided a strong stimulus for the recognition of the political and social rights of women. In the following years, many countries introduced women's suffrage and the social emancipation of women became an urgent theme on the agenda of international, governmental and non-governmental organizations.

Women's emancipation was constantly opposed by many distinguished thinkers. The ultra-radical Friedrich Nietzsche, who had proclaimed the 'revaluation of all values', curiously displayed an ultra-reactionary attitude with regard to women. In this respect he remained a disciple of that fervent misogynist, Arthur Schopenhauer. In *Also sprach Zarathustra,* in the section headed "Von alten und jungen Weiblein", Nietzsche declared that a real man wanted two things: danger and sport. He desired woman because she was the most dangerous of toys. Men were to be educated for war and women to be the recreation of the warrior. The chapter ends with the famous advice: "If you are going to have to do with women, don't forget your whip." It is very clear that while there was a place in Nietzsche's vision of the future for the Superman, there was no place for the Superwoman.

As long as the women's movement had been focused mainly on the battle for social and political rights, women with very diverse conceptions of life could cooperate. They might disagree about method, but they had the same immediate objective. Now they had to consider whether the winning of the vote, and other changes in their status, had really led to a true emancipation. The answer of course depended on the definition of emancipation, and that definition depended in its turn on prior choices of an ideological, philosophical or religious nature.

It seems to me that, in the worldwide discussion of the subject, four conceptions of emancipation have played major roles. The first was the idea that the emancipation of women was intended to ensure that they would enjoy the same political and social rights as had already been granted to men. The problem of inequality could be solved by appropriate legislation. By now many countries have progressed a long way towards that goal. After having determined directly or indirectly the legal situation of women for many centuries, the *patris potestas* which had, in most Western countries, given the *pater familias* such extraordinary power over his wife as well as over his children, had at last been abolished. Human rights are at last understood to be the rights of both men and women. It is interesting that the United Nations Commission which elaborated the 1948 Universal Declaration of Human Rights was presided over by a woman, Mrs Eleanor Roosevelt.

Many women and even more men believed then that the problem of the emancipation of women was to all intents and purposes solved. To be able to vote, to have access to most professions, to receive adequate salaries for their work, was this not all that could be asked? It was recognized that there was still a great deal to be done to ensure that the principles which had been accepted were in fact applied in less developed countries, but the governments were seen to be moving in the right direction. Some people were however asking whether the recognition of social and political rights had changed the situation in any fundamental way. These people came to propose a more radical conception of emancipation.

This second conception of the term involved a demand for total liberation from all traditional norms and values in the relations of men and women. Emma Goldman, who played a considerable role in the anarchistic movement in Russia and the United States, wrote in 1917: "Merely external emancipation has made of the modern woman an artificial being... Now, woman is confronted with the necessity of emancipating herself from emancipation, if she really desires to be free... They thought that all that was needed was independence from external tyrannies; the internal tyrants, far more harmful to life and growth — ethical and social conventions — were left to take care of themselves... If partial emancipation is to become a complete and true emancipation of woman, it will have to do away with the ridiculous notion that to be loved, to be sweetheart or mother, is synonymous with being slave or subordinate... It is this slavish acquiescence to man's superiority that has kept the marriage institute intact for so long a period... The sacred institution of marriage is gradually being undermined, and no amount of sentimental lamentation can stay it."[6]

These quotations are all the more interesting because they were written at a time when social and political emancipation was making progress, but had by no means been fully achieved. More and more women experienced disappointment, because the new freedom had not made as much difference as had been expected.

It was still a man-made world. "Women", wrote Simone de Beau-voir in 1949, "are on the whole still in the situation of vassals. It follows that women know themselves and choose themselves not in the light of their own existence but in the light of man's defini-tion of them."[7] The great re-evaluation of the ethics on which the relations between men and women had been based was therefore essential and, since the subjection of women had found its stron-gest expression in marriage and the family, it was necessary to abolish those antiquated institutions in their present form and replace them by new structures. The revolt against marriage and the family was, of course, not a new thing. We can find evidence of it in the Middle Ages and at the time of the Renaissance. In the nineteenth century, the early French socialists and the Russian anarchists had waged war on the traditional conception of mar-riage. It was, ironically enough, from the city of Geneva, which had known the strictest control of family life in the time of Calvin, that in 1868 Bakunin proclaimed his anarchist programme, which included the abolition of the *patria potestas* and of marriage.[8]

Nineteenth century literature was of course full of attacks on marriage and the glorification of free love. Shelley formulated this very clearly: "A husband and wife ought to continue as long united as they love each other. Any law which should bind them to cohabitate for one moment after the decay of their affection would be a most intolerable tyranny."[9]

But the philosophers, social reformers, novelists and playwrights who advocated total freedom in sexual relations had not yet suc-ceeded in seriously undermining marriage and the family. My par-ents' generation read the books of Ellen Key, Arthur Schnitzler, Anatole France and Guy de Maupassant. They saw the plays of Ibsen, and the less serious operettas of Offenbach, all of which called in question the institution of marriage. Somehow, however, these works did not affect very deeply the lives of the readers or the theatre-goers.This was, I think, to a considerable extent due to the fact that they did not recognize themselves in the heroes and heroines for, in spite of all that had been said about the hypocrisy and emptiness of bourgeois marriage, a great many men and women of that generation felt that, whatever problems they might have had in their own married life, marriage was for them still a tremendously positive force. When I ask myself how many of the marriages which I knew among relations and friends were the kind of prison described by the opponents of the state, I must answer that they were very few. In this respect I am inclined to agree with Dietrich Bonhoeffer, who thought that the time had come "to rehabilitate middle-class life as we know it in our own families" and began in his cell to write a novel in this spirit.[10]

Both anti-moralists and moralists make the mistake of considering marriage in terms of the moral 'rules and regulations' inherent in it. Lifelong monogamous marriage is far more than an instrument for the preservation of the moral structure of society. Today, when partners in a genuine marriage remain faithful to each other, in spite of the many opportunities for infidelity, it is not primarily because of the rules imposed upon them. It is due rather to an instinctive or conscious awareness that they do not want to lose or spoil a relationship which is their greatest blessing. Modern fear of marriage is a sign not so much of emancipation as a blindness to the true nature of human relationships. Statements like "Marriage is so definitive", "We prefer to stay together as long as we love, not as long as we live" and "We do not want to be committed" are often heard. It is, however, precisely this unconditional, mutual commitment which makes lifelong marriage unique, and it is the strength of the covenant between the two partners that gives it its meaning.

A modern marriage begins with *eros*, the attraction between two people, but true steadfastness and real union requires the addition of *agape*, a deeper, faithful and continuing love. A marriage in which both *eros* and *agape* find their place is the most precious human relationship. The widespread tendency today, even in the churches, to treat as only relatively important the difference between lifelong marriage and temporary relationships means that the younger generation may be largely unaware of the true value of the deeper bond which is one of the greatest treasures bestowed upon humankind. Novels, plays and films, and society gossip, have said enough about marriages which failed. It is time to speak of marriages in which men and women, with deep gratitude, have found each other.

The third conception of the emancipation of women emphasizes the unhindered manifestation of specifically feminine qualities and values which have so far not found sufficient expression. Those who think this way feel that the socio-political liberation of women is not enough, and see the next step as the working out of a feminine counter-culture. They believe that, if women do not become aware of their own identity, emancipation will lead simply to assimilation in the masculine world. The realization of such a feminine identity takes time, however, and can be achieved only through a temporary 'exodus' from their present cultural framework.

We find this exodus in an extreme form in the radical feminism of Mary Daly's book, *Beyond God the Father, Toward a Philosophy of Women's Liberation*. According to this philosophy, sexism, the oppression of women, is 'the root and paradigm' of all forms of oppression. Mary Daly's conception of history is, as it were, a feminine counterpart to that of Karl Marx. Marx spoke of one class, the proletariat, as the class which is *par excellence* the class of emancipation.[11] Mary Daly affirms that "the feminist movement is potentially the source of real movement in the other revolutionary movements."[12] Women, she asserts, have the right to say: "We are the final cause." In Marx's philosophy, there is a Messianic class; in Mary Daly's, there is a Messianic sex.

This form of feminism is also a counterpart to Nietzsche's philosophy. It rejects the Judeo-Christian tradition as Nietzsche does, but it draws a different conclusion. Zarathustra, speaking of the coming lordship of the higher man, said "God is dead, let the Superman live", and it is clear that this *Übermensch* is an *Übermann*. Mary Daly announces the departure of the Father-God to make room for the Superwoman. In this thinking, there is no room left for Jesus Christ, and no need for his presence is felt. To those who maintain that Jesus was a feminist, her answer is, "So what?" — as women do not need an example, or a saviour, in particular they do not need a male saviour. This form of feminism is against all traditional religions, declaring as it does that "Sisterhood is anti-church", and asserting that there is no other eternal 'Thou' than 'Being'.

Thus, real feminism and the Christian faith are asserted to be incompatible, for the real feminist is here defined as a person who does not accept that Christ reveals God and that this God is the Father God. It promises a 'cosmic upheaval', but an upheaval which, it seems to me, could easily lead to intolerable loneliness for men and women alike. Mary Daly's book is, in fact, a feminine monologue recognizing no dialogue. Indeed, dialogue would be impossible to those sharing her views, for it is impossible to hold a dialogue with the present participle of a verb, "Being".

Even if it is maintained that it is not possible to be at the same time a Christian and a feminist, it would be a tragic error for Christians to neglect the emancipation of women. So many social and cultural traditions of a patriarchal or even mysogynistic nature have been introduced into our 'Christian' civilization that a thorough reconsideration of Christian thought on the calling of women has become urgently necessary. Paul Evdokimov, an Eastern Orthodox theologian, in his valuable book *Women and the Salvation of the World* has commented thus on the sayings of the Church Fathers about women: "It is easy to understand the profound trouble which many sayings of the doctors of the Church may create in the sensitive souls of women, although these sayings come from men of recognized spiritual authority."[13]

Although theologians today do not give utterance to such wholesale condemnation of women as we have in earlier writings, most of them are men, and think in male categories. It is therefore a good and necessary development that recent years have seen a beginning of new and serious reflection on the vocation of women and the specific spiritual gifts which they can and should contribute to the life of the church and the world. This new feminist theology helps us to understand that the Bible contains not only a patriarchal tradition but also a prophetic critique of that tradition. Jesus in his frequent encounter with women proved to be wholly free from any prejudice which allocated a subordinate role to women, and reflection upon this fact opens up even wider horizons.

If, however, there is in the new theology the possibility of true insight into the role of the feminine in the Christian faith, there is at the same time the danger of grave error. Catherina Halkes, who lectures on "Feminism and Christianity" at the University of Nijmegen in the Netherlands, describes the task ahead in the following words: "Feminism is more than the liberation of women. It is also a critique of the present culture and religion. This religion has, because of the domination of the patriarchal and masculine experience, lost contact with profound realities which have found expression in older, archaic cultures: relatedness with the earth, rootedness in the soil, integration in the *Kosmos,* in water, air and in the heavens."[14]

If, as some modern feminists believe, this search for a more feminine spirituality means that we must bring back the Mother Goddess of the ancient religions, this will lead only to a superficial syncretism. The battle fought in biblical times between faith in a personal and holy God and the worship of the goddesses of fertility is not just past history, but has validity for us today. The very strength of the Judeo-Christian tradition depends on the maintenance of the prophetic tradition, a tradition which does not exclude the feminine, but which must resist any return to nature worship.

As Catherine Halkes has rightly pointed out,[15] we need the dimension of transcendence with its criticism of the closed world of the fertility religions, for it is precisely this transcendence that brings liberation.

It was not patriarchalism but the encounter with the living God which made Israel reject the fertility religions. It needs to be remembered that, in the nature religions, women were not respected as persons, but regarded as the source of mysterious sexual power. In our own time we have had in D. H. Lawrence an advocate of the 'dark religions' of cosmic consciousness. As to what happens to women who choose to live such a cosmic existence, we have in *The Woman Who Rode Away* Lawrence's description of the state of mind of a woman who leaves her over-civilized existence and seeks to find a new, a cosmic identity among primitive people: "She lived on in a kind of daze, feeling her power ebbing more and more away from her, as if her will were leaving her. She felt always in the same relaxed, confused, victimized state." And it must be asked, is that emancipation?

On the other hand, feminist thinkers make a most timely contribution with their concerted attack on the one-sided masculine character of our society and church life, and with their demand to be allowed to bring their specific gifts into the community. They are particularly qualified to help rid society of a number of 'tyrannies', such as its obsession with technological success, the intellectualism of much of our education and the impersonal nature of our institutions. In the churches, where women are often the most numerous and faithful members, decision-making is still wholly or largely in the hands of men. By bringing about a renewal of church life through their participation, women could make of the church a true fellowship of men and women.

One field in which women could, indeed do, play a leading role is that of the battle against the disastrous exploitation of nature. There is surely a link between the ideology of the domination of nature and that of the domination of women. To point this out is to prepare the way for an attitude to nature in which respect for the created world and concern for its health and conservation may act as a brake on acquisitive masters of nature. The emancipation of women and the new ecological awareness are two forces in the modern world which are related in depth and could together go far towards creating a viable society.

The fourth conception of the emancipation of women is that of ensuring that the relationship between men and women shall be one of genuine partnership and fellowship in freedom. The weakness of the first three which we have discussed is that they do not take seriously enough the fact that the root problem is not that of giving women the same status as men but that of the relations between them. Our thinking has long been influenced by philosophies in which the Ego, or 'I', was central and little attention was paid to interpersonal relations. Further, the conception of man was based entirely on a study of the male human being. When the philosopher Fichte declared that the world was a projection of the 'I', Heinrich Heine asked: "What does Madame Fichte think about this? Does she also believe that she exists only in the imagination of the ideal energies of her husband?" It never occurred to the great egoists that the 'ego' at the centre of their thinking could equally well be female. It was for this reason that my wife chose as the title of one of her articles: "Towards the Funeral of the Solitary Male."

In the years immediately following the First World War, a number of thinkers advanced into uncharted territory, as represented by the 'I-Thou' philosophy. As they began to concentrate on relations between persons as distinct from relations between persons and things, they understood that they were dealing with an absolutely essential and sadly neglected dimension of human existence. Karl Heim wrote in 1931 that this approach would lead to a new beginning in European thought.[16] Among the spokesmen of the new philosophy, Martin Buber was the most influential. When I had the privilege of visiting him in Jerusalem, I felt that I was in the presence of a genuine representative of the ancient tradition of Jewish wisdom. His small book *I and Thou* which appeared in

1923, unique in its combination of psychological, philosophical and religious perspectives, was an eye-opener to many and by no means only in philosophical circles.

By showing that there was a fundamental difference between the relation of the human person to the world of things ('I') and that of the human person to fellow-human beings ('Thou'), and that the centre of existence is the encounter between the 'I' and the 'Thou', he inspired many to review current thinking about the human person which had been dominated largely by the individualism of the idealistic philosophers. That all real life is a meeting between I and Thou and that this is a completely mutual experience now became the common teaching of philosophers as far apart as Gabriel Marcel and Karl Jaspers, and of theologians as different as Friedrich Gogarten, Karl Heim, Emil Brunner and Karl Barth. It was also the belief of J. H. Oldham, who translated the works of Buber into English, and of Dag Hammarskjöld, the Secretary General of the United Nations, who was reading and translating *I and Thou* when his plane crashed in the African jungle.

This school of thought had of course a very considerable influence on the understanding of the relations between men and women. Buber showed this when he made a sharp distinction between the 'broken-winged Eros', which is monological, and the true Eros which seeks a dialogical encounter. It is only when men and women really intend to accept one another as beings whose otherness they respect that they receive the reward of fellowship. This is vitally important, especially in marriage, the commitment which supports us as no other can.

Karl Barth was a pioneer in applying the 'I-Thou' philosophy to the relations between men and women. In the first volume of his *Church Dogmatics* published in 1945, when he came to deal with the doctrine of the creation, he gave a new interpretation to the first chapters of the Book of Genesis, according to which man was conceived as a being who was incomplete without a partner. He received "an help meet for him", or better his vis-à-vis, because it was not good that he should be alone. This, writes Barth, means that the partnership between man and woman is the fundamental human relationship, its Magna Charta. Man "needs a creature that is similar to himself but also different, in whom he can recognize himself, but not only himself, a being that is for him 'Thou' as surely as he is 'I' and for whom he is himself 'Thou', as surely as he is himself 'I'.[17] This conception was more fully developed in the later volumes of this work, which appeared in 1948[18] and 1959.[19] It is not too much to say that, in these passages, Barth expressed nothing less than a theology of the relations between men and women such as had never been heard before. Woman was no longer seen as an appendix to man, or as a second-class creature, but as sharing with him the vocation to fulfil the deepest intent of divine creation. Marriage was accorded a deep meaning, not simply as an institution for producing children, but as the most complete fulfilment of the encounter between I and Thou.

Had Barth then given up his insistence on the subordination of women which had been such a stumbling block to my wife? He continued to defend St Paul's ideas on this subject, though he went out of his way to express man's superiority in less absolute terms. He said that St Paul had not implied male tyranny or female subservience, but meant that women realized their humanity most fully by accepting men's leadership and initiative.

In 1948, when the First Assembly of the World Council of Churches was being prepared, it was decided that one committee should discuss "The Life and Work of Women in the Church". Although very few had read the heavy volumes of Barth's *Church Dogmatics,* it had become known that he had original ideas on the subject to be discussed. He was therefore invited to take part in the work of the above committee. The discussions were not easy. Most of the members of the committee were women in leading positions in Christian organizations or in the world of education. They had hoped that the Assembly, as a new departure in the life of the churches, would speak out against male domination in church life. What they heard from Barth seemed to them simply a new version of the old story. In the short time at our disposal, it appeared that Barth was merely advocating submission by women, in a slightly new form. It was not understood that he was first and foremost a pioneer in considering positively true dialogical relations between men and women. His reaction unfortunately was to make fun of those women who seemed to him to 'rush towards equality'. When my wife read his sarcastic remarks, she wrote to him that she was saddened by the fact that, while he had played an eminently constructive role in nearly all sectors of the Assembly, he had acted so negatively in the discussions on women. She reminded him that when she had asked whether the church had to be patriarchal, he had emphatically replied 'No', yet did not seem to realize that the churches were in fact strongholds of patriarchalism. She went on to say: "And it is not the will of God that women, by becoming subservient to their male partners in the alliance, become servants of patriarchalism." Barth visited us in Geneva, and peace was restored. On the issue of the subordination of women they agreed to disagree.

I however became increasingly convinced that my wife was right, and that while the Pauline ideas on this subject were a reflection of a pastoral concern very natural in the situation in which Paul lived, they were not of permanent validity. My wife continued to preach what Barth had called the Magna Charta, that the man-woman relationship was the fundamental model of co-humanity *(Mitmenschlichkeit)* in God's relations with his creatures. She wrote in one of her last articles that in a world still dominated by man, women's task was "to learn to distinguish between monologue and dialogue, to unmask false dialogue, to discover even the smallest attempt at true dialogue and to encourage it."

8. Youth seek emancipation from authoritarian fathers (patris potestas)

There is no evidence of youth movements, that is movements of young people affirming their ideas and desires over against the older generation, before the nineteenth century. If we ask why youth remained so long quiescent, students of historical psychology answer that, in a certain sense, there was no youth. J. H. van der Berg, in *Metabletica*, quotes one of them, Ph. Aries, as stating bluntly: "Youth is one of the great inventions of the eighteenth century." Till that time, society, and especially family life, had been so organized that there was no place for a period of adolescence with a life of its own. The child was admitted into the world of adults before there had been time for it to develop a youthful style of life. In the second half of the eighteenth century, however, family ties became less strict, the general growth of individualism gave young people a new self-consciousness and youth made its triumphal entry into literature. Rousseau's *Emile* led the way. Strangely enough, this explorer of the world of youth refused to be a father to his own children, and thus became a pioneer of the fatherless society.

There followed a series of novels and dramas in which the rebellion of young people was glorified. Addressing himself in his later years, Goethe said:

> Du hast getollt zu deiner Zeit mit wilden
> Dämonisch genialen jungen Scharen.[1]

His *Werther* was a sensation everywhere. Schiller followed with *Die Räuber* and more particularly with *Don Carlos* which highlighted the conflict between father and son, and was marked by a passionate insistence on freedom of thought. Early in the next century, Britain produced some of the most powerful advocates for liberty and against oppression, and they were all young. All other reasons aside, Byron and Shelley found the atmosphere of their country so oppressive that they preferred to live abroad.

These angry young people however did not yet form a coherent movement. The first attempt to organize youth and to elaborate a common programme for them was made in Germany. This might have been because German young people had heard of the new freedom of thought in other countries, such as the United States and France, and felt that the time was ripe for change in Germany too, with its reactionary régime. The *Burschenschaften,* loosely organized associations of young people which arose after the Napoleonic era, did not have very clear goals, and at first the movement displayed a somewhat primitive mixture of ideas. When its first great national meeting was held in 1817, the young people threw into the bonfire both wigs, and books propagating absolutist government, showing that they wished to break with the past and its ideas, to devote their lives to the making of a new world. As the movement grew, however, the authorities became nervous, and the murder of the dramatist Kotzebue by a student for ridiculing the *Burschenschaften* gave the government the pretext to forbid the movement and to apply sharp censorship on the spread of its ideas.

In 1848, the Year of Revolutions, students in Vienna gave an amazing demonstration of the power which youth can exercise if it has a clear purpose in view. Young people succeeded in bringing down the government of the so far all-powerful Metternich who, for forty years, had embodied the oppressive, anti-democratic policies of the Holy Alliance. This still remains, perhaps, the greatest political victory ever won by youth. When Metternich resigned, he said: "I am he who was." Though this was a moment of triumph for the Viennese students, their victory was short-lived. The reactionaries had, of course, control of the army, and the youthful revolt was put down by force. Among those who believed that the effort had been worthwhile, even if it did not succeed, was Karl Marx, who "was inordinately proud that Germans had given to the world such an example of revolutionary resistance."[2]

Like waves at flood tide, however, youth movements continued despite this setback. One of the heroes of the young was Guiseppe

Mazzini, who organized not only a movement called 'Young Italy' but also a 'Young Europe Society'. Guiseppe Mazzini, deeply involved in Italy's struggle for liberty and unification, was considered by various authorities to be one of the most dangerous revolutionaries of the time. In fact he was a great idealist who believed deeply in the moral evolution of humanity and taught that this evolution demanded the liberation of oppressed nations.

Young Christians also became active in the same period. In 1855, an international conference was held in Paris, where ninety-seven young men from seven countries decided to create the World Alliance of Young Men's Christian Associations. The YMCA soon became a worldwide movement. Towards the end of the century, a young American layman, John R. Mott, founded the World Student Christian Federation which brought new life to churches in many countries, and prepared the way for the ecumenical movement of the twentieth century.

The most radical protest of youth against the older generation occurred in Russia, where that most patriarchal of civilizations produced the most vehement anti-patriarchal outburst. Turgenev's novel, *Fathers and Sons,* published in 1861, described the chasm between the world of the fathers and that of the sons. The sons called themselves nihilists, and from then on 'nihilism' entered the international vocabulary. As to what nihilism is, the young men in Turgenev's novel stated that they did not recognize any authority, that the moment had come to destroy and deny everything so as to make room for whatever might come next. And when the older generation protested that, for the Russian people, traditions were sacred, and that they were a patriarchal people who could not live without faith, the nihilists answered that they demolished because they had the power to do so, and that power repudiated responsibility.

Turgenev was a keen observer, for in the following decades nihilism, which had at first seemed to be an intellectual pastime, developed into anarchism and terrorism and led to a whole series of murders of prominent people, including no less than six heads of state in the twenty years preceding the First World War. An important tenet of the creed of anarchism was that *patria potestas* had to be abolished. According to Michael Bakunin, paternal power was one of the pillars of the state, and it inevitably created a situation of slavery.[3]

In the last years before the 1914-18 War, a remarkably spontaneous youth movement arose, again in Germany. This was, of course, a reaction against the oppressive atmosphere of the Wilhelminian era, with its self-complacency, its materialism and its superficial culture, but the movement was not, in the first place, political. The first sign of this endeavour of youth was the *Wandervögel*, young people who took to the roads, many of them opting out of the social climate of their fathers which had become intolerable to them. When in 1913 these *Wandervögel* and other groups of what had come to be called the *Jugendbewegung* met on a mountain, the "Hohe Meissner", they demanded complete autonomy, declaring solemnly that they wanted to take responsibility for their own lives and with inner sincerity to seek their own destiny. For "youth is not simply a time of preparation, but has its own specific value, its own beauty and therefore the right to its own life, to the opportunity of developing its own nature."[4] But instead of creating the new world of which they had dreamed, the young people of the *Jugendbewegung* found themselves in the midst of a brutal world war.

After the First World War, youth movements in Germany did not regain their earlier momentum. In other parts of the world, for example in the United States and the United Kingdom, many young people turned against the power politics, social injustice and oppressive discipline of the established order. This 'revolt of modern youth' raised a demand for the right to freedom, including freedom in sexual relations. These young people were also strongly pacifist, their slogan being 'No more war'. In 1932, when the great Disarmament Conference was held in Geneva, young people in many countries expressed their concern and, at the opening session of the conference, a group of leaders of youth movements transmitted a petition on behalf of a very large number of young people to the participating governments.

Once again, however, the movement towards the emancipation of youth was arrested. In 1932, I addressed an international conference on the changes which had taken place in the situation of youth between 1927 and 1932. I said: "The youth of 1927 was largely characterized by an individualistic attitude to life. Freedom to live one's own life was the great slogan. Youth was deeply impressed by the theories of Bertrand Russell, André Gide and a host of authors who demonstrated the degrading influence of all super-personal norms and conventional standards and preached the gospel of self-expression... In an amazingly short time, however, this situation has changed radically. The somewhat self-conscious and self-centred youth of some years ago, who shrank from definite commitments and political and social decisions, has made way for a generation which joyfully sacrifices its individual judgment in order to identify itself with great causes and great leaders ... Youth of 1932 is tired of freedom. It wants powerful leadership, an object for devotion and opportunity for sacrifice."[5] They did not realize that many of the great causes and leaders would bring them to a catastrophe.

Four years later, I had occasion again to report on recent developments among youth. I pointed out that the mass movements had by that time become the decisive and dominating force. The young realized that they had no future unless there were a radical change in the social and international order, so they sought refuge in these mass movements which promised a new world. At the same time, these movements helped them to overcome the feeling of solitude and lack of meaning created for them by modern secularized society.

It is true that, in those same 1930s, there was also a remarkable renaissance of the Christian youth movements. The World Christian Youth Conference, held in Amsterdam just before the outbreak of the Second World War, was an impressive affirmation of the faith that in *Christus Victor* and not in totalitarian political movements, young people would find the answer to their search for meaning in life.

After the Second World War, the generation which, when young, had participated in the war through membership of armies or resistance movements, or who had suffered from it, found the post-war era deeply frustrating. Had so many sacrificed their lives or happiness for such meagre results? They were, however, too busy trying to reconstruct their own countries and their own careers to take any strong action. When I visited universities in many countries during the 1950s, I complained often that students seemed strangely docile and not much concerned about social and political issues.

It was the next generation, those born after the war, who became vocal in the 1960s and raised the flag of emancipation again. Karl Shapiro wrote in 1961: "Throughout the world, the human right of insubordination against industrial society, colonialism, militarism, and against the entire cult of the Western Tradition (religious, sexual, esthetic) is making itself felt in a thousand ways. The governments are losing their young. The lifeblood of history is flowing away from the centres of force."[6] Nobody, however, anticipated an explosion such as the series of youth revolts of 1968 which, starting in Berkeley University in California, spread all over North America and a large part of Europe, and found its climax in the wild days at the Sorbonne and the Odéon in Paris. This time, youth had really succeeded in shaking the establishment to its foundations. Imagine their feelings when they heard that President de Gaulle had left the Elysée to seek the protection of the army. And why did President Johnson decide not to run again in the presidential election of 1968? I have heard one of his collaborators explain that the main reason was the rejection by the younger generation of his policy in Viet Nam.

Intoxicated by the titan cocktail mixed by that excellent barman Herbert Marcuse, which contained the vodka of Marx, the wine of Nietzsche and the liqueur of Freud, the young participants in the revolt had never felt so happy. They expressed this by fighting the police and writing graffiti on the walls. "It is forbidden to forbid"; "Already ten days of happiness"; "I am a Marxist of the Groucho tendency"; "Be realistic, ask for the impossible"; "Respect is disappearing, don't bring it back"; "Forget all you have learned, begin by dreaming"; "Run, comrade, the old world is behind you"; "The general will against the will of the general"; "Neither master nor God — God, that's me"; "What is a master, a God? Both are an image of the father and fulfil by definition an oppressive role" — such were the ideas of the students as inscribed on the walls of the universities.

It was clear that the students would not be content with a partial success in the field of university reform, but were determined to bring about a total revolution in culture. They therefore made serious attempts to arrive at an alliance with the workers. However the distance between those whose struggle is, in the words of the revolutionary student leader, Cohn-Bendit, "about the hierarchical structure of society, about oppression in comfort" and those who "suffer from direct economic oppression and misery" proved to be too great to be bridged. This cultural revolution of the young therefore did not bring into being that new world of which they had dreamed.

This is unlikely to be the end of the story of the emancipation of youth. The 1968 battle for a complete cultural revolution was lost, but there will be further battles. In the meantime, the young are developing their counter-culture. In communes of various kinds, in festivals of their music, in pilgrimages to seek Eastern gurus, in protest movements against pollution and technocracy, and in other ways, many of today's young people are seeking to build up a culture based on the total rejection of the values of the established order, and are trying to elaborate a life-style of their own. Theodore Roszak, who has analysed this counter-culture as it appeared in 1968, says about the United States: "So, by way of a dialectic Marx could never have imagined, technocratic America is producing a potentially revolutionary element among its own youth. The bourgeoisie, instead of discovering the class enemy in the factories, finds it across the breakfast table in the person of its own pampered children."[7] The same is true of many other countries. As Roszak points out, it is possible that this counter-culture will not have any lasting result, and will prove to be only a temporary fashion, "a hopeful beginning that never becomes more than a beginning." But it is also possible that it will prove to be a stage in the preparation of a real transformation of culture. The question still remains unanswered.

9. The struggle for emancipation from ecclesiastical paternalism

The strongest religious influence in my school and university years came, not from the church, but from the Student Christian Movement, which was an independent body. In its camps, conferences and study groups, no distinction was made between theologians and lay people. Some of the most impressive of the evening talks at the summer camps were given by laymen, who might have had difficulty in expressing themselves, but who spoke so simply and directly that their words went to our hearts.

When I left university, I joined the International Secretariat of the World Alliance of Young Men's Christian Associations and, a few years later, I became General Secretary of the World Student Christian Federation. Thus, during the first fourteen years of my professional life, I served in movements which, although connected with the churches, were not directed by them. I should add that, among the men who have guided me in the orientation of my professional life, there have been more laymen than clergy or theologians. I have the impression, therefore, that I have lived on the frontier between the lay world and the world of the clergy.

These experiences have led me to the belief that the problem of the role of the laity is not simply one of discovering how to use them more effectively in church life. To be sure, as Hendrik Kraemer has emphasized, lay people are the 'frozen assets' of the church and their mobilization is essential to its well-being. But this mobilization must at the same time be an emancipation. If it does not permit lay people to make independent, responsible decisions with regard to their Christian task in the world, then the problem is not solved.

Let us first consider the historical development of this question. The church described in the New Testament believed in the priesthood of all believers, and its church order was of a very flexible nature, in which there was no sharp division between office-bearers and other church members. Soon, however, a clear distinction developed between clergy and laity. We see the conflict between the two conceptions in the life of Tertullian, the Carthaginian theologian who lived in the second century A. D. While he was still Orthodox in his beliefs, he insisted that laymen should not perform the function of the priesthood. When he joined the Montanist sect, however, he wrote: "Are not we laymen priests also?... for where there are three, there is a church, though they be laymen." However, the clergy became increasingly men apart, and the central figure in the official church was the bishop. We generally speak of the rise of the monarchical episcopate. That is correct insofar as the bishops became more and more the leaders who had final and complete authority. It would be more appropriate, however, to speak of the rise of the paternalistic episcopate, for few bishops would have wished to be considered as monarchs, but all of them wanted to be respected as fathers with full *patria potestas.*

Thus Ignatius, writing early in the second century A. D. to the Christians in Magnesia about their bishop, said: "It is not right to presume on the youthfulness of your bishop. You ought to respect him as fully as you respect the authority of God the Father." In the Apostolic Constitutions of the fourth century A. D., the role of the laity is described in the following words: "The layman should honour the good shepherd (the bishop), respect him like a father, lord and master, as the high priest of God, as a guide in piety." It goes on to state that laymen should sit in their places quietly and in a seemly manner.

When, after Constantine, the church had to assume responsibility for the religious and moral life of the whole of society, its attitude to the masses of superficially evangelized Christians became increasingly paternalistic. St Augustine came reluctantly to the conclusion that those who refused to obey must be treated to an "active process of corrective punishment." For him, God was a stern Father who treated his children with strict discipline. Thus the first step was taken which was to lead to the coercion of heretics by violent means.

In the conflict between the spiritual and the secular powers, the paternal nature of the church was an important argument for its domination over temporal rulers. In the eleventh century, Pope Gregory VII wrote: "Who can doubt but that the priests of Christ are to be considered the fathers and masters of kings and princes and of all the faithful? ... If we are ordered to honour our fathers and mothers after the flesh, how much more our spiritual ones."[1]

The paternal character of the church order was intensified with the rise of the papacy. In the first centuries of our era, many clergymen were called 'Papa' or 'Pappas', that is, 'father'. From the eighth century on, however, the Bishops of Rome considered this title as exclusively attached to the See of Rome. The Pope became the father *par excellence* or the father of fathers. In 1177, the peace treaty concluded between Pope Alexander III and Emperor Frederick I stated that the Pope and the Emperor would support one another, "the Pope as the kind father of his pious and dear son and most Christian Emperor; the Emperor as pious son and Christian Emperor his beloved and venerable Father and Vicar of St Peter."

When Popes were crowned with the triple tiara, the liturgical text was: "Take the tiara and know that you are the father of princes and kings, the ruler of the world, on earth the vicar of our Saviour, whose honour and glory is eternal." This terminology was by no means rhetorical. It expressed the conception on which papal decisions were based, and which determined papal attitude to the laity. Boniface VIII, in the Bull, *Clericis Laicos,* stated: "Not content with what is their own, the laity strive for what is forbidden and loose the reins of unlawful things."

The laity reacted in various ways to clerical paternalism. The conflict between the Popes and the Emperors was not merely a political struggle about power. It was also an ecclesiological conflict about the nature of the church. The Papal case was strong insofar as it defended the freedom of the church. It was weaker insofar as the interests of the church were identified with the temporal power of the papacy. At a different level, there was the reaction of various sects and movements which protested against clerical omnipotence or even rejected the hierarchy altogether. An old description of the Waldensian movement in North Italy and Southern France stated that Waldensians did not recognize the clergy, calling them blind leaders of the blind who did not hold to the truth of the gospel and did not imitate the poverty of the apostles.[2]

One of the most radical movements was that of a branch of the Franciscans who took their inspiration from Abbot Joachim of Fiore. He taught that there were three great epochs in the history of salvation. First, there was the epoch of the Father which was the epoch of the Law, that of the Old Testament. Secondly, there was the epoch of the Christian church with its priestly hierarchy, and thirdly, there would be the epoch of the Spirit, in which the hierarchical order would be supplanted by a common life of a monastic character based on worship and contemplation. These *Spirituales* as they were called, announced that this prophecy would find its fulfilment in 1260.

In the fourteenth and fifteenth centuries, when the papacy passed through a critical period, the voices demanding the emancipation of the laity grew stronger. Wycliffe and Hus challenged the established clerical order at many points. How critical opinion had evolved in the last years before the Reformation can be seen from *Praise of Folly* by Erasmus. In 1508, years before Luther began to oppose the papacy, Erasmus made his attack on the hierarchy. When he spoke of the Popes, it was not in a tone of humour, but one of indignation. He contrasted the Popes' titles, 'Father', or 'Holiness', with the reality of their lives and gave a realistic picture of the papacy in the Renaissance period. Speaking of excommunication, he wrote: "These most holy fathers in Christ and vicars of Christ use this weapon against all who seek to diminish the possessions of Peter." It is remarkable that a man who wrote in such terms about the hierarchy nevertheless became a highly appreciated counseller of the Vatican.

Luther did not merely criticize the abuses of the clergy, but raised the fundamental question as to whether the traditional distinction and separation of clergy and laity could be justified. One of his earliest works, *To the Christian Nobility,* is really an appeal to laymen in positions of leadership. In it he stated that the distinction between a spiritual estate and a temporal estate was a fiction, for "all Christians are truly of the spiritual estate." There was no difference between them save of office. When a clergyman was deprived of his office, he became "a peasant or a citizen like the rest."

As to the claim of the Pope to be the supreme judge in matters of faith, Luther stated that it was heresy to reduce the church to one man. "We are all priests and have all one faith, one gospel, one sacrament; how then should we not have the power of discerning and judging what is right or wrong in matters of faith?" Luther's hope that the church might come to embody this biblical concept of the universal priesthood was not fulfilled. There arose a new paternalism. The pastors and the civil authorities did not leave much more room for the laity than the bishops had done. Calvin found the solution in the offices of elder and deacon and thus created a counterweight to the ordained clergy. The Pietists renewed the church of Luther's original concern. Spener, their leader, emphasized again that all Christians belong to the spiritual estate and should teach, exhort and edify their fellows.

But the time of the large-scale emancipation of the laity had not yet come. It was in small groups or sects, such as the Quakers, that laymen were able to make their specific contribution. There were also a few outstanding Christian personalities who showed what a loyal lay opposition could mean and how it could enrich rather than weaken the church. I shall take as examples four very different men.

The first of these is Pascal, the greatest layman of his time. He devoted his life to the defence of the Christian faith. He desired to be a loyal son of the Roman Catholic Church, but had the courage to speak up when he felt that the church authorities were wrong. Thus in the nineteenth letter of his famous *Lettres écrites à un Provincial,* he stated that the doctrine of papal infallibility meant that believers had to become either slaves of the Pope or heretics.

The second of the laymen to be considered is Hugo Grotius, the pioneer of international law, who also contributed much to biblical exegesis and wrote a handbook on the Christian faith which was intended for the use of laymen, especially sailors. Although he was a victim of the intolerance of Reformed churchmen, he became an ardent advocate of church unity and counted Anglicans, Lutherans and Roman Catholics among his friends.

Third among our laymen is Rembrandt. At the time when a deeper spiritual dimension became visible in his work, he was in conflict with the church over his relationship with Hendrikje Stoffels, but he went forward on his spiritual journey, and his inspired interpretation of the 'Three Crosses' and of the Prodigal Son belong to the following years.

Then there was Zinzendorf, a German religious leader who established a fellowship of laymen. He had become convinced that Christians were called to a task of world-wide mission, but found that the churches were not willing or able to undertake the task. He therefore organized the Moravian missions, considering his community not as an alternative to the historical churches, but as a body called upon to pioneer for church unity.

These men were exceptional Christians, but they announced the arrival on the historical scene of the layman who would stand on his own feet, make up his own mind and, if necessary, take his own initiative.

The nineteenth century is of special importance in the history of the laity, for then lay people began to organize themselves into different groups and societies. They played an important role in the creation of many bodies, such as missionary and Bible societies and anti-slavery movements. They organized the YMCA, the YWCA and later the World Student Christian Federation. In a number of churches which had been largely or wholly run by the clergy, the laity claimed, and received, important roles in the governing bodies.

The nineteenth century was, however, also the century of *laicisme,* that is, of aggressive anti-clericalism. According to its partisans, emancipation would not be a movement within the churches, but would be a liberation from the churches. Freemasons and adherents of political liberalism attacked what they considered to be the tutelage of the church over society and culture. The papacy became so concerned about the dangers which the emancipation of the laity seemed to entail that it attacked the modern world in its entirety. *The Syllabus of Errors,* issued in 1887, summarized the many warnings against modernity given in papal declarations in recent decades, declaring that it was an error to think that the "Roman Pontiff can, and ought to, reconcile himself to, and agree with, progress, liberalism and modern civilization." At the same time, the decisions of the first Vatican Council, held in 1870, concerning the infallibility of the Pope and his universal jurisdiction made it absolutely clear that the Roman Church intended to maintain its patriarchal structure and paternalistic discipline.

The reaction of loyal Roman Catholic laymen to this development was well expressed by that very wise lay apologist for Roman Catholicism, Baron Friedrich von Hügel, who admitted that there was no recognized position or action of a directly spiritual nature left to the layman in the Roman Church. He immediately added, however, that a monopoly of all influence by the clergy was as un-catholic as to have no clergy, and no hierarchical subordination.[3] He defended the existence of the ecclesiastical institution and the necessity for official authority, but he also recognized that "church officials are no more the whole church, or a complete specimen of the average of the church than Scotland Yard, or the War Office, or the House of Lords, though admittedly necessary parts of the national life, are the whole, or average, examples of the life and fruitfulness of the English nation."[4]

One sphere in which laymen and laywomen played a very considerable part was the ecumenical movement, where most of the preparatory work was done by lay movements like the YMCA, the YWCA and the World Student Christian Federation. Among the pioneers of the movement the proportion of laymen was considerable. Most of the young men who founded the World Alliance of YMCA in 1855 were laymen, among them George Williams, the English social reformer, and Henri Dunant of Red Cross fame. The World Young Women's Christian Association, created soon afterwards, attracted to its leadership many able and devoted women who had little opportunity of serving the churches.

After 1895, when the World Student Christian Federation was founded, a network of relationships between Christians of many countries came into being, which was very largely due to the efforts of laymen and laywomen. It has become customary to consider 1910, the year of the World Missionary Conference in Edinburgh, as the beginning of the modern ecumenical movement. It is however historically more accurate to go back at least another fifteen years. The expression 'ecumenical movement' was not in general use until the large church conferences of Stockholm and Lausanne, but in these earlier ecumenical stirrings we already find the characteristics which mark the modern ecumenical movement as a new factor in the history of the church. There was the experience of meeting Christians who differed greatly from those in one's own church but with whom one felt deeply united; there was the awareness of belonging to a world fellowship, and the comfort of mutual encouragement in word and deed. University students in the first three decades of this century were able, through the World Student Christian Federation, to acquire a vision of the Church Universal. The YMCA, YWCA and WSCF were not only lay movements in the sense that they were independent of the churches, but also because laymen and laywomen played a decisive role in their life. For example, during the first forty years of its existence all the successive chairmen of the WSCF were laymen.

Perhaps the most influential layman of that time was John R. Mott. The question as to whether he can really be called a layman can be answered in the affirmative, because his activism and his practical way of thinking had much more affinity with the approach of the laity than with that of theologians. In this early period, Dr Mott exerted an extraordinary influence in the many countries which he visited as an evangelist and missionary statesman. As the generally recognized leader of the WSCF, of the YMCA and, a little later, of the international missionary movement, he was able to prepare the soil for the growth of the ecumenical movement. Looking back on the role which the WSCF had played, Dr Mott described it as "practice games in weaving together the nations and the communions."[5] One of his books was entitled *Liberating the Lay Forces of Christianity* and that is exactly what he was engaged in. He used to say that he owed a debt to all Christian traditions, and he inspired many to work for church unity.

His colleague, Miss Ruth Rouse, became the first woman secretary of the WSCF in 1904, when women students were still looked upon as a strange phenomenon. She succeeded in obtaining recognition for women in the WSCF, so that it became customary to choose the best person for a job, regardless of sex. She also served as President of the World YWCA.

Members of the WSCF received their first impression of the new forms of Christian spirituality coming into being in Asia and Africa through outstanding laymen and laywomen from these continents who attended Federation meetings. There was K. T. Paul of India, the YMCA leader who later became a vice-chairman of the WSCF. He understood the significance of the Indian national movement, advocated a far-reaching Indianization of the life of the church and was an active and critical participant in the movement for unity which led to the creation of the church of South India.

When K. T. Paul represented the Indian Christians at the Round Table Conference in London in 1930, his colleague at the Conference was Dr S. K. Datta, an educator and leader of the Christian community in India. He had represented India also at the meeting in 1921 at which the International Missionary Council was founded and later joined the staff of the WSCF.

Dr T. Z. Koo brought to the WSCF conferences a glimpse of Chinese Christianity. He had originally been a railway official, but had accepted an invitation to do Christian work among students. In 1922, Dr Mott asked him to visit the Indian Student Christian Movement and, after that, for the next twenty-five years, Dr Koo served the Federation as an evangelist, visiting almost all parts of the world and, with the help of his flute, spreading his simple, straightforward Christian message and interpreting the spiritual contribution which China could make to it.

From Japan came Dr Nitobe, an interpreter of Japanese culture who became a prominent official of the League of Nations, and from Africa came Kwegyir Aggrey, the educator who had represented African Christians at the foundation meeting of the International Missionary Council. As a student, I heard him say that, just as you cannot play a piano without both the black and the white keys, so you cannot carry on the work of the world without both the black and the white races.

The laity played an important role also in the encounter between Eastern and Western Christianity in the 1920s. I am thinking especially of Russians who came to live in the West, like the great philosopher Nicolas Berdyaev, his colleague Zenkovsky, Leo Zander and Nicholas Zernov, all of whom helped the West to discover and to respect Eastern Christianity, and to learn from it.

Many remarkable lay persons stimulated the ecumenical movement in its early days. One who explored new possibilities was the Quaker, J. Allan Baker, a British Member of Parliament. He led a deputation to the second peace conference in The Hague in 1907, and presented a memorandum on arbitration signed by church leaders in Europe and the United States of America. Later, he became chairman of an organization set up to foster friendly relations between the British and the German peoples through the churches, and, in August 1914, at the very moment when "the lights were going out" all over Europe, he presided over the first conference of the World Alliance of Churches for Promoting International Friendship.

After his death in 1918, another British Member of Parliament continued his work. Sir Willoughby Dickinson became Honorary Secretary and later President of the World Alliance for Friendship through the Churches, an organization which was one of the most dynamic expressions of the ecumenical movement between the two World Wars.

Robert Gardiner, a Boston lawyer, became the first Secretary of the 'Faith and Order' movement in 1910. From that moment until his death in 1924, he devoted his whole time and energy, and a good deal of his money, to the creation of a wide network of contacts between the churches and succeeded in awakening the interest of Protestant, Anglican, Orthodox and Roman Catholic church leaders in the cause of church unity.

A most unexpected contribution to the ecumenical movement was made by Sir Henry Lunn, a Methodist who was the director of a tourist agency. Through his Swiss contacts, he was able to invite guests to hotels in such beauty spots as Grindelwald and Mürren, and in fact discovered the latter as a tourist centre. There he assembled leaders from different churches for informal conferences, at which a number of ecumenical initiatives were born.

Lucy Gardiner represented the Society of Friends, the Quakers, at the 1920 meeting of 'Faith and Order'. As one of the two executive secretaries of the British Conference on Politics, Economics and Citizenship, held in 1924, she helped to prepare the way for the 'Life and Work' Conference held in Stockholm in 1925. Through her appointment to the Executive of the Continuation Committee of the Stockholm Conference, she became the first woman to break through the barrier of masculine domination in the ecumenical movement.

It was natural that a movement which owed so much to laymen and laywomen should be concerned about the place of the laity in the church. The man who become the indefatigable advocate of lay participation was J. H. Oldham. It was due to his skill in convincing prominent lay people that the ecumenical cause was not just a hobby for ecclesiastics but a cause of fundamental importance for the whole of our civilization that, at the Oxford Conference, so many statesmen, economists, jurists and others participated in the drawing up of the reports by the five sections of the Conference, and that three of these five sections were chaired by laymen. It was also Oldham who, at that time, wrote the following sentence in the first outline of the plan to create a World Council of Churches: "The witness which the church in the modern world is called to give is such that in certain spheres the predominant voice in the utterance of it must be that of lay people holding posts of responsibility and influence in the secular world."

When the World Council of Churches finally came into existence at Amsterdam in 1948, its Assembly stated: "Only by the witness of spiritually intelligent and active laity can the church meet the modern world in its actual perplexities and life situations." The second Assembly, held at Evanston in 1954, in its report on "The Laity: the Christian in his Vocation", laid a firm foundation for a fruitful discussion on the 'theology of the laity' which was carried on in the following years, through the WCC's newly created Department of the Laity, as well as through the *Kirchentag* movement in Germany, led by Reinold von Thadden, and through kindred movements in other countries.

All these movements had in common that they desired a true emancipation of the laity, one with the definite purpose of making lay people true witnesses in an increasingly secularized world. All shared the conviction that in modern society the lay witness should have the widest possible ecumenical dimension. A number of Orthodox thinkers made a unique contribution to the discussion about the place of the laity in the church. They took their stand on the old principle of the Eastern Church which had been restated in 1848 in the Encyclical Letter of the Eastern Patriarchs, to the effect that the guardian of orthodoxy is the body of the church, that is, its individual members. In their view, the West's mistake had been to think in juridical terms rather than in the terms of the *koinonia* or fellowship (in Russian, *sobornost*) which is characteristic of the church of Christ. These representatives of the Eastern church believed that, when the church had been a Christ-centred community, the laity was fully integrated in it, and could therefore play an active role as members of its councils.

In the last hundred years, the Roman Catholic Church produced a number of outstanding laymen and laywomen, who won for it a strong position in culture, politics and society in general, but little thought was given to the theological problems raised by the question of the place of the laity in the church and of the vocation of lay people in the world. The appearance in 1953 of Father Yves Congar's book *Jalons pour une théologie du laïcat* was therefore a remarkable event. For the first time, the basic issues regarding the laity were thoroughly and comprehensively analysed, and an attempt was made to give positive answers of importance for the future. It is of course impossible to summarize this great work, but it can be said that Father Congar sees in the life of the church two principles: the hierarchical principle and the principle of community or fellowship. The church can exist in its fullness only when the two principles are brought into a living synthesis. He wrote that in the history of the church, far more attention had been paid to the hierarchical principle, and expressed his belief that the time had come to enrich the church by stressing its character of fellowship through demonstrating the importance of the laity to the life of the church and its witness in the world. This book appeared at the right time, for although it seemed to be a solitary voice when it appeared, it in fact became a signpost on the road to the Second Vatican Council.

In the light of church history, it was of very great significance that the Second Vatican Council paid careful attention to the 'Apostolate of the Laity', a theme never before discussed in the councils of the Roman Catholic Church. It soon became clear that there was a very great divergence of opinion in the Council. While Cardinal Ruffini said bluntly that the hierarchy had to command and the faithful to obey, Bishop de Smedt of Belgium declared that neither adults nor young people in our time wanted to be treated as children. No laymen participated in the work of the drafting committees, but in some cases their opinion was sought and some lay groups put forward suggestions. For example, an American group led by Michel Novak informed the bishops that "many people see in the church not the People of God, but an ecclesiastical society of clergy, and of laymen who obey the clergy." The chapter on the laity in the "Dogmatic Constitution on the Church" and the "Decree on the Apostolate of the Laity" which resulted from this long process of elaboration and correction are very substantial documents, and answer many questions about the place of the laity in the church and its task in the world. An American bishop exclaimed that "laymen had waited four hundred years for these documents."

In the Dogmatic Constitution, the calling of the laity is described in very positive terms. "They are in their own way made sharers in the priestly, prophetic and kingly functions of Christ." Clergy and laity "all share a true equality with regard to the dignity and to the activity common to all the faithful for the building up of the Body of Christ." The document further states: "The lay apostolate is a participation in the saving mission of the church itself." Thus it would seem that the church was now seen as a fellowship of believers in which the only differences were those of function, and in which there was no place for paternalism. It is therefore a little disconcerting to find later in the same document a number of statements which seem to issue from another, more traditional school of thought. According to these statements, lay people are those who "receive the spiritual goods of the church." They should accept with ready Christian obedience whatever their pastors, the sacred representatives of Christ, decree in their role as teachers and rulers in the church. We find a typically patriarchal image in the bishop who considers 'with fatherly love' the projects, suggestions and desires proposed by the laity.

Thus it can be seen how difficult it is to foresee the full consequences of the realization that the laity is not the object of the church, but the church itself. The main problem is that it is not possible to give the laity the place it is entitled to occupy according to the new ecclesiology unless the clergy makes room for them, that is to say, unless the clergy is willing to share with the laity responsibility for the life of the church. This inevitably raises the question of the participation of the laity in the making of decisions and in the government of the church. However at the time of the Council the moment to reach a positive decision on this had not yet come, and the bishops stated again that the episcopal order and its head, the Roman Pontiff, enjoyed full and supreme power over the universal church. In matters of faith and morals, the bishops spoke in the name of Christ, and the faithful were to accept their teaching and adhere to it with a religious assent of soul. The task of interpreting authentically the Word of God, whether it is written or handed down orally, had been entrusted exclusively to the living teaching office of the church.

So, in spite of a genuine desire to treat the laity as responsible, fully adult members of the church, the paternalistic note inevitably recurs. The bishop had the office of father and pastor. "Let him be a true father who excels in the spirit of love and solicitude for all and to whose divinely conferred authority all gratefully submit themselves."[6] The faithful had to realize their obligations towards their priests and ought to follow them as shepherds and fathers, with filial love. One of the reasons for maintaining the obligation of celibacy for priests was that it made them more able to exercise paternity in Christ.

In recent papal declarations also we find a return to a more paternalistic terminology. Pople John Paul II, in his Letter of 1979 concerning the priesthood, also defends the necessity of celibacy with the argument that by denying themselves human paternity, priests seek another paternity, the relationship of the spiritual father to his spiritual children.

In the meantime, the lay world is less and less willing to accept that these spiritual fathers know better than their children what is best for them. In a remarkably balanced article in *Theology Today* of January 1980, the Jesuit professor John A. Coleman calls attention to the growing cleavage in the Roman Catholic Church between the 'official' church and the majority of the faithful who are seeking pastoral help in solving their problems rather than answers imposed by authority. These people do not leave the church, but try to form a 'loyal opposition' within it.

Thus the battle for the emancipation of the laity in the Roman Catholic Church is by no means over. The situation is in some ways easier in the Orthodox, Protestant and Anglican Churches because the paternalist factors in their tradition are counterbalanced to a greater degree by elements which are anti-authoritarian. These churches too, however, have not yet solved the problem of allowing the laity the place to which, according to the very nature of the church, it is entitled.

10. Emancipation from paternal morals

In one sense, all problems experienced during the process of emancipation are moral problems. We have therefore already dealt with several aspects of the tensions which arise when a group seeking emancipation rejects the moral criteria of the established authorities. It is not superfluous, however, to pay more specific attention to the question of opposition to dominant moral conventions, for we must try to find out whether we are dealing with an effort to correct and reform certain moral customs or with a fundamental attack on the whole moral system on which our civilization is based.

It is not surprising that in history morals have always been linked with tradition. Societies seeking to defend themselves against a variety of dangers desire cohesion and continuity. These can be found only if the social order is based on a consensus concerning moral standards, which must be dependable and durable. Morals are therefore passed on as one of the most treasured gifts which a generation can give to its successors.

Ancient Israel and Rome, both of which have deeply influenced Western civilization, each in its own way developed its concept of morals as the truth by which the ancestors, the 'fathers', had lived. The well-being of the people depended on faithful adherence to these concepts, which had therefore to be transmitted in the purest possible form to each new generation.

The fifth chapter of the Book of Deuteronomy, which records the proclamation of the Ten Commandments, is followed by one in which Moses repeatedly warns the people that these Commandments are to be kept not only by the generation of the Exodus, but also by their sons and their sons' sons. "And these words which I commend you this day shall be upon your heart; and you shall teach them diligently to your children and shall talk of them when you sit in your house, and when you walk by the way, and when you lie down, and when you rise."[1] Similarly, according to the Psalmist, God established a law in Israel "which he commanded our fathers to teach to their children, that the next generation might know them, the children yet unborn, and arise and tell them to their children"[2].

Israel had its vocation and identity as the people to whom the will of God had been revealed in the Torah. The faithful were therefore expected to give priority to the study of the law of the fathers. This did not necessarily take the form of painstaking casuistry. The prophets of Israel were interpreters of the deeper intentions of the law and taught that keeping it was to stand for righteousness in all domains of life. It remains true, however, that the decisions concerning the moral life, the choice between right and wrong, had been taken once and for all when the Covenant between God and the Children of Israel was made.

In Roman civilization, there was also a strong emphasis on the traditional nature of morals. The *mores* which all Romans had to maintain and defend were the *mores maiorum,* the moral convictions and customs of their ancestors. The poet Ennius wrote in the second century B.C.: *Moribus antiquis stat res Romana virisque,* which we may translate: "The strength of Rome depends on the ancient moral standards and on the quality of its men." Cicero's comment on this line was that in its brevity and exactness it seemed to have been uttered by some religious oracle. For the true reason for the greatness of Rome was indeed that it had produced a number of outstanding men who had maintained ancient *mores* and ancestral institutions.

Roman authors with a sense of responsibility for the life of the nation therefore constantly appealed to their compatriots to return to the style of living of the good old times, when men and women made great sacrifices for the common good. The historian Sallustus drew special attention to the words of Cato, who had said that it was not through the force of their arms that the ancestors of the Romans had created a great republic out of a small city. The real reason for its rise to greatness was the moral attitude of those early generations. Similarly, Horace, writing at the time when

Augustus was seeking to bring about a moral and religious renaissance, also spoke of 'mores of gold', that is to say, those which represented the standards and customs of the Golden Age. The highest praise which Horace could give to Augustus was that he was bringing back the ancient morality. In his famous 'Carmen Seculare', written at Augustus' command for the Secular Games, Horace spoke of "truth, peace, honours, ancient chastity, neglected virtue" as 'returning' to Rome. Virgil in his poems and Livy in his Histories aided greatly in the elaboration of a philosophy of history according to which the future of the nation depended on the rediscovery of its moral heritage.

Let us now consider how this conception of morality as tradition and heritage was affected by the teaching of the Christian church. Jesus had not come 'to abolish the law',[3] but he had given a new interpretation of its nature and meaning. Every part of the law had to be understood in the light of the two central Commandments to love God and to love one's fellow human beings.[4] This radical concentration and simplification meant that moral actions were no longer described in terms of commandments, but rather in terms of personal relations. God spoke to men through Jesus himself. He was as it were the Torah in person, and to follow him was to lead the good life. Believers were not called upon to make their moral decisions like lawyers who seek to find out which specific legal ordinances are applicable in any given case. They were to decide as did children who were in close contact with their father who loved them and desired them to become channels for his love to their neighbours.

St Paul elaborated this, stating clearly that the law given to Israel was summarized in the great commandment to love one's neighbour and that love was the fulfilment of the law.[5] Those who had heard God's call in Christ were no longer under the law, but followed a 'more excellent way', the way of love.[6] God's love had been poured into our hearts[7] and we are able to pass it on. The law had had the function of a custodian[8] but now that believers were enabled to live according to their true vocation, the time of emancipation had come. Christ offered them a glorious freedom. True morality was not achieved by observing moral rules but by living in communion with Christ. Paul could therefore say that he was not without law, but was under the law of Christ or, as the French ecumenical translation puts it, that Christ was his law.[9] Although

Christians were no longer bound by the law, it was still of significance for them in that it indicated what loving God and loving
one's neighbour meant. Paul could therefore use examples from
the traditional law in his exhortations concerning the life of the
Christian community[10], and he himself continued to keep the traditional commandments.[11]

The question as to whether the Christian church was thus really
emancipated from paternal and traditional morality cannot be
answered by a simple yes or no. In fact, three different types of
morality must be considered. One can be described as neo-
legalism. In this view, Jesus was a teacher of the new law,[12] a law
enriched by his teaching, but not essentially different from the old
law. St Paul's theology which rejected the law as a way of salvation but respected and upheld it as a signpost on the way of the
Christian seeking to express God's love in Christ was hardly one
for people who wanted simple answers to simple questions.

For a long time, the Old Testament was the only holy scripture
available, which meant that Christians were constantly confronted
by traditional morality. The Ten Commandments continued to be
used in liturgies and catechisms as containing the quintessence of
morals, but very important elements of the teaching of Jesus about
human relations were not transmitted in the same way, as for
instance concern for the poor, the need to forgive and to love
one's enemies. Thus a very large part of the Christian community
was not emancipated in its moral life, but accepted moral standards defined for them by their spiritual leaders.

It is true that St Paul's appeal, "For freedom Christ has set us
free, stand fast therefore and do not submit again to a yoke of
slavery"[13], also found enthusiastic supporters. But had they really
understood what Paul meant by freedom? Many of them had a
very different conception of emancipation from that of St Paul. A
typical illustration of the misunderstanding is the use made of the
statement "All things are lawful." We find it in two passages in the
First Epistle to the Corinthians[14], and in each passage it is repeated
twice. It is therefore clearly a statement which was well-known to
the Corinthians and which had been used either in the discussions
which Paul had had there, or in the correspondence exchanged
since his visit. For this reason, many modern translators put it in
inverted commas, as for example in the Revised Standard Version
of the Bible, and in Lietzmann's *Handbuch zum Neuen Testament*.

This is also done by Wendland in *Neues Testament Deutsch,* by the *Traduction oecuménique de la Bible* and by James Moffat.

In the original Greek, the statement has the sharpness of a slogan or a battle cry. It is an emphatic protest against paternalism. Its revolutionary character is not sufficiently clear in the English translations. The German *Alles ist erlaubt* as in the Zürich translation and in the N. T. Deutsch or the French *Tout est permis,* as used by Segond and in the Version Synodale, and by the *Traduction oecuménique* would seem closer to the original, and the rendering 'Everything is permitted' would be preferable in English.

But who was the author of this assertion? Commentators and translators give two different answers. A number of scholars, including Karl Barth and Paul Feine, believe that it expresses the conviction of St Paul himself. Is it then a statement which St Paul had made in Corinth and which the Corinthians now used to defend their moral freedom before him? According to J. B. Philips in *Letters to Young Churches,* Paul wrote: "As I have said before, the Christian position is this: I may do anything."

However, Calvin and Grotius had earlier expressed the opinion that these words were a Corinthian saying quoted by St Paul. Many modern commentators take this view and believe that the words 'everything is permitted' had been important in Paul's discussions in Corinth, or that they represented a quotation from a letter addressed to him by the Corinthians. The translators of the New English Bible are so strongly convinced that the phrase is a Corinthian slogan that they take the unusual liberty of adding the words: "You say...", so as to make it clear that the words are not to be attributed to Paul. There are similar additions in Today's English Version and in the German "Gute Nachricht".

Which interpretation is right? It seems to me most probable that it was a Corinthian saying, for while it is difficult to imagine these words coming from Paul, they can easily be explained as a Corinthian idea. Paul had certainly spoken in strong terms about moral freedom, but whenever he spoke of freedom, he made it clear that he was not referring to arbitrary licentiousness, but to the freedom of people whose lives were rooted in and directed by God's love as made manifest in Christ. When St Augustine wrote "Love and do what you like", he was a true interpreter of St Paul. However, St Paul with his pastoral sense was clearly aware of the harm such a position could do if the word 'love' was omitted. For Paul, everything was permitted only within the specific context of the life of faith. All was permitted, provided that it was motivated by divine *agape* or spiritual love. The struggle between that love, and the motive of self-assertion continued, said Paul, throughout life, and people had to be reminded constantly what Christian love really meant. In the sixth and in the tenth chapters of the First Epistle to the Corinthians, Paul made sure that the saying 'All is permitted' should be understood in its proper context.

On the other hand, the statement emerged naturally from the ideas of that group in Corinth who were discussed and condemned by Paul in those chapters of the First Epistle to the Corinthians which deal with the resurrection. In *Nachgelassene Schriften und Aufsätze,* Julius Schniewind has sought to analyse the theology of these Corinthians, and concludes that it represented an early form of gnosticism. These Christians believed that they had reached the stage of true knowledge (gnosis), and that they were therefore no longer part of the old world. Their physical existence was, they believed, an illusion and of no importance, so that nothing was forbidden to them. St Paul and these Corinthians both spoke of freedom, but in fact there was a great gulf between them.

When gnosticism became a strong and widespread movement, we find again the same radical rejection of morals. One wing of the movement was ascetic, but another taught that just as filth has no power to damage, so the spiritual person could not lose the spiritual substance, whatever material action he or she might take.[15] Clement of Alexandria quoted the gnostic Prodicus as saying that those who had the true knowledge were lords of the Sabbath and royal sons far above the rest of mankind, and that no law was prescribed for a king.[16] Gnostic ideas also penetrated into the Islamic world. In the eleventh century we find the strange sect of the Assassins, the followers of the "Old Man of the Mountain", Hussan ben Sabbah, whose esoteric principle was "Nothing is true; everything is permitted." Since these Assassins had, on various occasions, been in contact with members of the Order of the Knights Templar during the Crusades, some historians believe that this anti-moral doctrine became part of the secret teaching of the Order and was one of the reasons for its tragic downfall. This has, however, never been proved.

It was during the Renaissance that a widespread movement of protest against traditional morals dared to manifest itself. One of its most telling spokesmen was François Rabelais. In a famous passage in chapter 57 of his *Gargantua*, he described the Abbey of Thélème, his ideal of the good life. He listed some of the characteristics of the life of the Thelemites: "All their life was spent not in laws, statutes or rules, but according to their own free will and pleasure. In all their rule, and strictest tie of their order, there was but this one clause to be observed: Do what thou wilt. Because men that are free, well-born, well-bred and conversant in honest companies, have naturally an instinct and spur that prompteth them to virtuous actions, and withdraws them from vice, which is called honour." Jacob Burckhart said that this statement of Rabelais represented a turning point in the history of culture.[17] For this was the first public confession of a purely secular type of amoralism. Everything was permitted for those who had the right social background and the right education. The freedom of the Christian was replaced by the freedom of the *honnête homme*, "who can read, write, sing, play several musical instruments, speak five or six different languages and compose in them all very quaintly, both in verse and in prose."

This manifesto was written at Lyon and was published in 1532. Its demand for a society which would not impose traditional paternalistic morals, but would leave men free to express themselves in whatever way they desired, seemed at the time to be just a wild and dangerous dream. In the same years, Calvin was writing his *Institutes* which were to become the basis for the establishment of the strictly disciplined society of Geneva. He considered the new freedom as described by Rabelais to be an attack on the very foundations of society. He wrote: "What is going to happen in the end, if everybody is permitted to live as he wills?"[18] The Abbey of Thélème remained a chimera and the theocracy of Geneva became a reality, but Rabelais had achieved a break-through. The 'libertines' who were at the same time free-thinkers and opponents of traditional morality, were to grow in number and in influence.

In the next century, the tension between the libertines and the political and religious establishment became clearly visible when Molière produced his *Dom Juan* in 1665. In this play, the sharp-tongued servant, Sganarelle, demands of his master, Dom Juan, whether he really believes that, because he belongs to the *beau monde,* and is well-dressed with an elegant wig and feathers in his hat, therefore 'everything is permitted' to him. But Dom Juan does not heed him, for he is obsessed by the thought of his next love-affair. Molière was sharply criticized for presenting on the stage a "school of liberalism and of atheism". After a few performances, the play was banned and did not appear in print. Louis XIV had not forgotten the line which he had to copy as a child: *L'hommage est du aux Roys, ils font ce qu'il leur plaist. Louis.*[19] A Dom Juan must not behave as if he were a king. It is perhaps not without significance that Louis's copy book later became part of the autograph collection belonging to the Russian Imperial Family.

When we come to the eighteenth century, we find Denis Diderot, the editor of the famous 'Encyclopedia', an author who made a thorough study of the revolt against traditional morality. Some time between 1761 and 1774 he wrote a short novel, *Le Neveu de Rameau* which, however, he did not publish. The Encyclopedia was, in his own words, a contribution to the spread of knowledge and the increase of virtue. Considerable confusion would have been caused had he published at the same time a book in which the chief character makes the most convincing apology possible for a total moral relativism. The mansucript came into the possession of Catherine the Great and was clandestinely copied. Schiller came across it and, in 1803, he sent it to Goethe, who was so impressed that he translated it himself. Hegel made considerable use of the book in the chapter on morality in his *Phenomology of Mind* (1802). Curiously, until 1823, the only available French text was a re-translation from the German of Goethe.[20]

Le Neveu de Rameau made such a deep impression because Diderot described this rebel against the morals of his society as a man who had worked out a coherent philosophy of immorality, had the courage to live by it, and the sincerity to proclaim it. Diderot makes him say: "Moreover, bear in mind that in a matter as variable as behaviour there is no such thing as the absolutely, essentially, universally true or false, unless it is that one must be what self-interest dictates — good or bad, wise or foolish, serious or ridiculous, virtuous or vicious.... When I say vicious, it is by way of speaking your language, for if we came to a clear understanding it might turn out that what you call vice I call virtue, and that what I call vice you call virtue."[21] This seemed at the time to be an astounding liberation. In spite of the fact, therefore, that this strange hero finds lying and cheating perfectly normal, men of the quality of Diderot, Goethe and Schiller were deeply interested and did not conceal their sympathy for him. Hegel went even further, considering that the nephew's struggle for freedom was a stage in the development of a higher level of conscious life, though it remains quite unclear where in Diderot's novel Hegel found any indication of an approach to or awareness of that higher consciousness.

In the nineteenth century, the anti-moralist becomes a familiar figure. Schiller's 'Karl Moor', Goethe's 'Faust', Byron's 'Don Juan', Balzac's 'Rastignac', Stendhal's 'Julien Sorel' and a host of other heroes of the novel or the theatre had in common that they were moral revolutionaries, and that their efforts to escape from the prison of traditional morals had a heroic quality.

In the realm of philosophy, Ludwig Feuerbach, who in the revolutionary year of 1848 became a popular leader of the younger generation, taught that "all that a man can do to satisfy his instincts is permitted."[22]

Max Stirner went even further than Feuerbach. He preached the gospel of radical egoism and became the spiritual father of individual anarchism. In *The Individual and his Property*, written in 1845, the individual was the overriding reality. Stirner taught that a person had the right to do anything of which he was capable. The fact that he was capable of taking possession of something authorized him to make it his property. One had the right to be what one wanted to be, if one had the force to realize the goal. One had to deal with the world according to one's instinct, not according to one's ideals.

Stirner's ideas exerted a considerable influence on the Russian nihilists. It is almost certain that Dostoevsky's description of Raskolnikov's philosophy in *Crime and Punishment* was largely based on Stirner's book.[23]

Radical amoralism was translated into action by Nechayev, who murdered one of his former associates. This murder forms the historical background of Dostoevsky's *The Possessed*. Nechayev's *Catechism of the Revolutionary*, written, strangely enough, in the city of Calvin, Geneva, was based on the principle that in the service of revolution, anything was allowed. "For a revolutionary, everything is moral and valuable which promotes his chief aim."

The outstanding author who made the question, "Is everything permitted?" a central theme in his novels was Dostoevsky. He however showed the rebels against morality as victims of an illusion rather than as heroes, and made a frontal attack on nihilism. Raskolnikov wanted to prove that he did not belong to the ranks of the ordinary people who had to live according of the official rules of morality. He felt that he belonged to a small elite which was not bound by these rules. He was fascinated by Napoleon, of whom he said: "A real master, to whom everything is permitted, bombards Toulon, organizes a massacre in Paris, forgets his army in Egypt, spends half a million men in Russia, and in Vilna, when questioned about it, dismisses it all with a pun. And it is to this man that they erect statues after his death. Thus everything is permitted." On this theory, Raskolnikov murdered a pawnbroker whom he considered as a worthless being, but the theory did not work. After the murder, Raskolnikov was not the free, emancipated hero, undertaking great tasks. He was the victim of his megalomania and egocentricity. The decision to commit the murder had been the product of his cold reasoning, but he discovered that, as a human being, he had to take other realities into account. He was then "tortured by the feeling of being separated and isolated from the community of human beings."[24] When Sonja, the prostitute who had remained pure of heart, helped him to rediscover what a truly human relationship meant, Raskolnikov decided to confess his crime to the police.

Is this the story of a Christian conversion? Not in the usual sense. Raskolnikov is clearly deeply impressed by Sonja's faith but he is not yet ready to repent. It is only in the last paragraph of the novel that Dostoevsky refers to Raskolnikov's future as "the story of a gradual renewal, of a gradual rebirth, the gradual transition from one world to another world, the encounter with a reality which had so far been completely unknown to him."

In Dostoevsky's last great novel, *The Brothers Karamazov,* the religious dimension of the question 'Is everything permitted?' becomes explicit. The sharply reasoning Ivan Karamazov questioned every generally accepted idea, and had worked out a theory that, when people ceased to believe in their immortality, they would cease to believe in a moral law and would conclude that everything was permitted.

Even criminal actions would become reasonable and inevitable. This seemed at first the wild idea of a young man who wanted to prove his originality and his daring, but it gradually becomes clear that Ivan is really obsessed by the dilemma: if God exists, then man is answerable to him and is not permitted to do anything he wants; if God does not exist, man may act according to his own free will. Ivan's brother, Dimitri, is deeply impressed by this theory, for he hates his father and asks himself whether Ivan's theory may not help him to overcome his reluctance to commit patricide. The servant, Smerdiakov, who is, as it were, a caricature of Ivan, has no scruples at all. When he murders old Karamazov, he feels that he is acting on behalf of the two brothers. In a letter quoted by Dominique Arban, Dostoevsky explains that Ivan's objection to the faith proclaimed and practised by Jesus was that he believed Jesus seriously to have overestimated the human being. Humanity could not possibly live in such freedom as Jesus had envisaged. Ivan had therefore invented the Legend of the Grand Inquisitor, who considers it his mission to improve the message and work of Jesus. The human being need not live in that terrifying freedom proclaimed by Christ, wanting as he did mankind to give itself whole-heartedly to the service of God. The Inquisitor offered an easier solution, according to which one need not take any decisions, since all questions of good and evil would be decided for people.

In the novel, Ivan receives a visit from a stranger who is really the diabolical aspect of his own personality. This Mephistopheles stressed once more that a new period of human history was in sight, in which people would rid themselves of faith in God and become gods themselves. This would take time, but those who had the new insight could already adopt the principle that everything was permitted. There is no law for the gods.

Ivan is right in that he protests against the system of the Grand Inquisitor, the system of imposed morality, for human beings are called to freedom. He is wrong in seeing no alternative other than the self-glorification of the human person. *Tertium datur,* there is a third way. It is the way taken by his brother Alyosha, the way of the divine love which makes people truly free.

Dostoevsky has shown that the principle that everything is permitted does not lead to freedom, but to new forms of slavery. The supermen described in his novels, who consider themselves to be above the law, are not guides to a higher and more abundant life, but seducers who lead the way to anarchy and catastrophe.

Dostoevsky died in 1881, two years before the appearance of the first parts of Friedrich Nietzsche's *Also sprach Zarathustra*. In his novels, Dostoevsky had given a preview of Nietzsche's philosophy of life, and had rejected its presuppositions. To those who have read Dostoevsky's novels first, it comes as a surprise that Nietzsche should call himself 'the first immoralist'. Similarly, his use of the slogan, 'everything is permitted' was not, as he seemed to think, a particularly original contribution to the discussion on morality. In *The Genealogy of Morals,* he wrote: "When the Christian crusaders in the East came across the invincible order of the Assassins, this order of freethinkers *par excellence,* whose lower members lived in an obedience such as no order of monks has achieved, they in some way obtained information about the symbolic and essential principle, the knowledge of which was reserved as a secret to the higher degrees: 'nothing is true, everything is permitted'. That was the real freedom of the spirit."[25] Karl Jaspers remarked that this principle, which Nietzsche has quoted with approval in a number of his writings, is meaningless if it is taken out of the context of Nietzsche's total philosophy of life, but it has the function of a polemical formula against attempts to treat truth as a possession, and seeks to ensure that man shall not cease to move forward in his search for truth.[26]

Nietzsche's total war against morals is based on the conviction that they are essentially a denial of life, which seek to obstruct the self-expression of the natural man. When Zarathustra speaks of the 'old and the new Tables' (of the Law), he says: "When I came to men I found that they had an old prejudice: they all believed that they had long known what was good and what was bad for mankind. All talk of virtue seemed to them an old and tedious business." Zarathustra has come to teach that the difference between good and evil is known only to the creative man, while the moralists 'crucify man's future'. Nietzsche was on firm ground when he fought in this way against the legalism of moralists for an ethic of spontaneity, but he is led astray by his conception of the Superman, the result of his denial of God's existence. Paradoxically, here the immoralist becomes a supermoralist. The source of new 'values', according to Nietzsche, was the 'will to power', and the new morality was the morality of an élite, of whom one of the best examples was Napoleon. It is however by no means certain that those whose lives are dominated by the will to power know true freedom, for the will to power is an obsession which can enslave us just as easily as any other human passion.

Nietzsche said that the advantage of his times was that nothing was true, and everything was permitted. The outstanding authors of the twentieth century have shown themselves in agreement with him. Anatole France's philosophical doctor says: "Morals are a matter of taste", and goes on to express the wish that the Academy of Moral Sciences would adopt this principle.[27] André Gide entitled one of his novels *L'Immoraliste,* and described in it his own struggle to free himself from the morals imposed upon him in his youth.

In his essays advocating life worship, *Do What You Will,* Aldous Huxley attacks all morals which limit self-expression. As an introduction to the book, he used William Blake's lines:

Do what you will, this world's a fiction
And is made up of contradiction.

For Huxley, St Francis was a model not of humility but of vanity, Dostoevsky's novels were absurdly unnecessary tragedies of selfmade madmen, and Pascal was a death worshipper. Huxley believed that men should at last discover that the purpose of life was more life. All have many selves, each of which has as good a right to exist as the others. In his opinion, this doctrine, which might seem dangerously subversive, was a doctrine for well-born and well-bred people, for, as Rabelais said, if one is well-born and well-bred one does not behave like a pig. In other words, everything should be permitted to those who had gone to the right school, the right university, and who, I may add, belonged to the right club. That this élite had been educated on the basis of a completely different morality does not seem to worry the author.

One of the most influential prophets of the revolt against traditional morality was Herman Hesse. Of his novel, *Demian,* published in 1919, Thomas Mann said that it had had an electrifying effect in the period just following the First World War, and had been deeply appreciated by the young. Hesse's novels also enjoyed a remarkable revival among young people in the USA and Japan during the ideological battles of the 1960s. In *Demian,* Hesse describes the emancipation of a student from the narrow moral world in which Jehovah is the law-giver to a wide and free world in which 'Abraxas' is the divine principle. Those who knew Abraxas "must not fear anything and must not look upon anything as forbidden which the soul in us desires."[28] Who is this Abraxas? It is the name given in the gnostic writings of the second and third century A.D. to a divinity which included the immoral, diabolical element in its own being. Hesse's message represents a renaissance of the gnostic teaching on freedom from moral restraint which St Paul found in Corinth and which were later detected in heretical sects by Irenaeus.

It seemed that the revolt against paternalistic morality had gone as far as it could but, when the students at the Sorbonne in Paris rose up against the Establishment in 1968, they added to the principle that everything was permitted the slogan: "It is forbidden to forbid." In this way, they weakened rather than strengthened the anti-moral position for, as Albert Camus remarked: "When no one can any longer say what is white and what is black, the light is extinguished and freedom becomes a voluntary prison."[29] Living means choosing and there can be no choice without the acceptance of values. Life without values is life thrown away. It was not a coincidence that the great poet, Charles Baudelaire, who made the revolt against morals the main theme of his work, was at the same time the poet of boredom. In the introductory poem of *Les Fleurs du Mal,* he warns his readers that he will confront them with all sorts of diabolical and monstrous powers that operate in the human soul, but that there is one power which is more evil than all the others:

> Il ferait volontiers de la terre un débris
>   Et dans un baillement avalerait le monde
> C'est l'Ennui.[30]

11. The revolt against the fatherhood of God

The various struggles for emancipation from fatherhood so far mentioned concern human relations. They often had a religious dimension, but the fatherhood of God was used sometimes as an argument for emancipation and sometimes as an obstacle to it. Thus, men and women who fought slavery did so in the name of God the Father, but Karl Marx and his followers could not conceive of an emancipation of the proletariat from oppression which would not, at the same time, be an emancipation from any conception of a divine father.

We must now consider the attempts to eliminate the fatherhood of God from the traditional Western cultural heritage. The first important name we come across in this connection is Spinoza. At first sight, he does not seem to be in revolt against the Christian conception of God as Father. In his *Ethica,* there is no direct polemic on the subject, but that is precisely what is astonishing about Spinoza. Having grown up as a Jew in a culture still firmly Christian, he suddenly produced an alternative faith and philosophy of life which was radically opposed to the Judeo-Christian tradition. He did not say explicitly that one must not think of God as Father, but he proclaimed a god whom he called *Deus sive natura,* 'god or nature', who was definitely not a father. Further, between the lines of his work can be read that he was defending his conception of God against the Jewish rabbis and Christian theologians who based their theology on the Bible. Spinoza taught that God cannot love or hate, for God has no emotions. Those who love God must not desire to be loved by him.[1] It is clear that such an impersonal God is the negation of the God of the Bible.

Spinoza's God does not call men and women to him, he does not act in history, he is not the eternal 'Thou' but a great 'It'. During Spinoza's lifetime, and indeed for most of the eighteenth century, his teaching seemed so audacious and radical that it did not have any great influence. By the time of the great cultural revolution of the end of the eighteenth century, however, his thought became one of the major forces in the building of the modern world. Lessing and Goethe became his disciples. Hegel called his philosophy the liberation of the spirit. A Dutch admirer praised him as the man who brought the good news that humanity had come of age.

In the eighteenth century, we find little open revolt against the fatherhood of God, but much scepticism and doubt. Voltaire, who stood at the very centre of the Age of Enlightenment, had at first spoken in favour of faith in God as "master, judge and father".[2] In 1755, however, when a terrible earthquake in Lisbon killed thousands of people, he initiated a great debate about divine providence:

> Mais comment concevoir un Dieu, la bonté même,
>   Qui prodigua ses biens à ses enfants qu'il aime,
> Et qui versa sur eux les maux à pleines mains?[3]

In William Blake, engraver, poet and mystic, we find two contradictory attitudes. He could write:

> For Mercy, Pity, Peace and Love
>   Is God, our Father dear,
> And Mercy, Pity, Peace and Love
>   Is man, his child and care.[4]

He was also, however, capable of a violent outburst against the divine Father: "Thinking as I do that the creator of this world is a very cruel being, and being a worshipper of Christ, I cannot help saying 'The Son, O how unlike the Father.' First God Almighty comes with a thump on the head. Then Jesus Christ comes with a balm to heal it."[5] Blake's famous frontispiece of 'The Ancient of Days' seems to confirm this gnostic theology, for it portrays the Almighty as the Demi-urge, the mysterious and frightening creator of all things.

Some years later, the young poet Shelley sang of the glory of total emancipation. He welcomes enthusiastically all the struggles for freedom which are going on, and in any anthology which might be made of the poetry of liberation would be found Shelley's ideas of revolt against priests and kings, against oppressive masters, and authoritarian fathers or husbands. In *The Revolt of Islam,* a long poem which he first intended to call "The Revolution of the Golden City: A Vision of the Nineteenth Century", he expressed his anger "at all the oppressions which are done under the sun" and welcomed "the unveiling of the religious frauds by which the people had been deluded into submission." Shelley affirmed that the rule of men over their fellowmen was derived from a belief in an omnipotent God:

> But children near their parents tremble now,
> Because they must obey — one rules another.
> And as one Power rules both high and low,
> So man is made the captive of his brother.

The main theme of Shelley's *Prometheus Unbound* is the revolt of the freedom-loving human being against Jupiter, in other words, the emancipation of the human being from divine fatherhood. In his preface, he stressed that he purposely changed the ancient story, where the tragedy ends with the reconciliation of Jupiter and Prometheus. Shelley did not want 'the champion of mankind' — Prometheus — to make peace with 'the oppressor of mankind', Jupiter. So in his version Prometheus overcomes Jupiter 'the tyrant of the world' and at last man is:

> Equal, unclassed, tribeless and nationless
> Exempt from awe, worship, degree, the king
> Over himself; just, gentle, wise....

So, as Shelley saw it, the one hope of humankind was to rid itself of its Father in Heaven.

By far the most serious and effective assault on the fatherhood of God came from that triumvirate of Titans, of insurgents against heaven who have had such a decisive influence on thought during the last hundred years: Karl Marx, Friedrich Nietzsche and Sigmund Freud. Can these three be compared in any way? Are they not utterly different men whose ideas are opposed to one another? They are indeed. If, about the year 1880, it had been possible to put them in the same room, they would have found it difficult to settle on a subject of conversation. Nietzsche was not interested in the proleteriat, Marx was not concerned about the Superman and Freud would have found both the others distressingly uninterested in dreams. However, if one of them had said: "Let us talk about the emancipation of the human being from traditional, paternalistic religious conceptions", then the other two would readily have agreed.

These three men belong together in the context of the revolt against the fatherhood of God. For all of them, this revolt had a high priority in their plan for cultural revolution. All were reformers who preached a warning about the nefarious influence of religion, and it was their combined impact on the thinking, first of the West and then of many other parts of the world, which made this attack the most dangerous which the Judeo-Christian tradition had yet had to endure.

All three believed that there was something fundamentally wrong with Western civilization and found that people sought to solve their problem of maladjustment by constructing an artificial mythology about a heavenly father who punished them for their sins. In his *Genealogy of Morals*,[6] Nietzsche wrote of man who had invented bad conscience. Man tortured himself with this sense of guilt because of his revolt against the father, the original ancestor, but this was to be regarded as a sickness. These ideas are reminiscent of Karl Marx's early writings where he calls religion a false consciousness, the illusion of happiness and the opium of the people. Later Freud, in his *The Future of an Illusion*, tried to prove that religion was a neurosis based on the human father-child relationship. All three men strove therefore to emancipate human beings from their dependence on an imaginary superhuman power. As Marx put it, it had to be discovered that "man is for man the highest being". He added: "To demand that we should reject our illusions concerning our own situation means to claim that we must reject a situation in which illusions are needed."[7]

These thinkers therefore found that people had to turn their eyes away from the other world and concentrate all their powers on their life on earth. Making this point in *The Future of an Illusion*, Freud quotes the following lines from Heine's *Die Winterreise:*

> Den Himmel überlassen wir
> Den Engeln und den Spatzen.[8]

In *Das Eselsfest*, in *Also Sprach Zarathustra*, the prophet accuses his disciples of becoming pious again, of praying as children do, saying 'Dear God'. He continues: "Indeed, if you do not become as little children, you will not enter the Kingdom of Heaven, but we do not want to enter the Kingdom of Heaven: we have become men — and we want the Kingdom of Earth."

The pioneers of anarchism went even further in their revolt. In their view, faith in God the Father was not merely an illusion or a malady, it was the source of all evil in current society.

Proudhon wrote that all progress was a triumph which broke up the divinity. He believed that the human attributes given to divine providence, such as father, king or judge, were nothing but caricatures of human life, incompatible with the validity of civilization. Thus the Father in Heaven became man's greatest competitor. Proudhon exclaimed: "Eternal father, Jupiter or Jehovah, we know you. You were, and always will be, envious of Adam, you will always be the tyrant of Prometheus."[9]

Michael Bakunin, the leader of the Russian anarchist movement, spoke in similar terms. "Evil", he wrote, "is the Satanic revolt against divine authority." In his view, evil had a positive function. "It is the fertile germ of all human emancipation."[10]

There was then among the intellectuals of the nineteenth century a growing consensus that the fatherhood of God was out of date. Even among those who did not become atheists and who still considered themselves to be religious, there were very many who eliminated all personal elements from their conception of God. Einstein is a good example of this. He was certainly a believer, but he wrote: "In the struggle for the good life, the teachers of religion should have the inward greatness to abandon the doctrine of a personal God. They should do away with that source of fear and hope, from which priests have in the past drawn such tremendous power."[11]

According to Albert Camus, the basic conception of modern thought was the need to transform *homo homini lupus* (man a wolf for his fellows) into *homo homini deus* (man a god for his fellows), but this could be brought about only by denying the fatherhood of God.[12]

We may conclude this chapter by looking at André Gide's version of the parable of the prodigal son.[13] The central figure of this is not the father, as in the New Testament, but the son who left his father's house because he felt it to be a prison and because he wanted to gain new experience. He returned, not because he wanted to come home, but because he was tired of the hard life in

the desert where he felt himself a captive, and was harshly greeted
by his father, urged on by the elder brother, who is now really the
head of the family. The father has become old and it is the elder
brother's view that the prodigal should not have risked anarchy by
breaking up the traditional pattern of the family. Gide added to
the characters in the Bible a still younger brother who asked if the
prodigal had returned because he was defeated. The reply was that
the prodigal had come back because of acquiescence to the fact
that he had lost the freedom he sought, and as a captive had had to
serve. The youngest brother, declaring himself a captive in his
home, prepared in his turn to leave. The last words of the prodigal
to him are: "Be strong. Forget us. Forget me. I hope you do not
come back." In this 'revised' version of the parable, it can clearly
be seen that the tragedy of all human attempts to revolt against the
fatherhood of God is that freedom has become an end in itself and
that the real father has disappeared.

12. Dimensions of emancipation

The bird's-eye view we have had of the process of emancipation from various forms of paternalism has revealed that emancipation is a universal phenomenon. It appears in all sorts of places and affects all sorts of people. Those engaged in the fight for emancipation are a motley crew. A portrait gallery of its advocates would show a great variety of people, probably unaware that they had anything in common, and would include Immanuel Kant and Peter Kropotkin, Emmeline Pankhurst and Victor Hugo, Dietrich Bonhoeffer and Guiseppe Mazzini, Martin Luther King and Jawaharlal Nehru. However, in mentioning these men and women from different backgrounds, each having a specific reason for engaging in the struggle against paternalism, we see clearly that as emancipation became universal, its nature and meaning became more and more diversified. Some day, a scholar with the encyclopedic knowledge and the power of synthesis of Ernst Troeltsch or Arnold Toynbee may make a thorough comparative study of its various manifestations, showing their common elements and their interaction. I can only make a few remarks on this fascinating subject.

The first impression gained is that emancipation is contagious, but emancipated groups or those being emancipated are often blind to the equal need of other groups. As we have mentioned, it did not occur to the pioneers of human rights that women and slaves should be included in their great vision. Many Dutch and French people resisted keenly the foreign occupation of their country, but were astonished to find that Indonesians, Vietnamese and Algerians were no less desirous to be free. Advocates of political freedom became alarmed when underprivileged groups raised the issue of freedom from economic exploitation. Many other examples could be given.

We have seen, moreover, that we must make a distinction between emancipation as a natural and peaceful coming of age and emancipation as a sharp conflict. The peaceful form can be compared to the situation in most societies when the transition from a state of tutelage to a state of adulthood is recognized. Young men and women at a certain age are made welcome in the company of mature adults, come to share their privileges and to accept their way of life. Emancipation through conflict, on the other hand, is a battle between those who feel that they are repressed and those who are not ready to grant them complete freedom. Thus, movements seeking liberation from patriarchal domination have in many cases become insurrections against the authority of the patriarchs.

Which form emancipation takes depends, to a considerable extent, on the attitude of the two parties. When those in authority seek to defend their right to command, and have no confidence in the group demanding independence, conflict is inevitable, as it is when those who seek emancipation consider that their opponents cannot possibly understand their claims and therefore discussion is useless.

This is not, however, simply a question of the presence or absence of good will on the two sides. It is far more a question of whether the nature of emancipation is understood or not. There are two conceptions of it which are entirely different and which create much confusion and misunderstanding if they are not clearly distinguished.

I shall illustrate this point by two quotations, both from reports issued by the Second Vatican Council. The Roman Catholic Church has been very suspicious of emancipation in most of its forms. It was therefore a moment of great importance when, in the "Pastoral Constitution on the Church in the Modern World" the *Gaudium et Spes,* the Council declared: "In every group or nation, there is an ever-increasing number of men and women who are conscious that they themselves are the artisans and the authors of the culture of their community. Throughout the world there is a similar growth in the combined sense of independence and responsibility. Such a development is of paramount importance for the spiritual and moral maturity of the human race." The document went on: "Thus we are witnesses of the birth of a new humanism, one in which man is defined first of all by his responsibility towards his brothers and towards history."[1]

This is a remarkably positive evaluation of the modern movement towards emancipation, but that does not mean that the Council approves of all such movements. In another paragraph of the same document, it said: "Many look forward to a genuine and total emancipation (Latin — *liberatio*) of humanity solely by human effort. They are convinced that the future rule of man over the earth will satisfy every desire of his heart" — but the report goes on to make clear that the Council considers this understanding of emancipation as a dangerous illusion.

Can the difference between the two conceptions of emancipation be defined more precisely? Both want all people to enjoy freedom and to live in community. According to the first, this goal is reached when all men and women are able to participate fully in a society which is a better edition of society as it is at present, one which would continue to maintain the same norms, but would apply these more seriously and effectively.

The second on the other hand is based on the conviction that the emancipation of the human being is impossible as long as the norms and structures of our present patriarchal society are maintained. The established order is by its very nature a system of paternalism and domination. The only hope, therefore, is to overthrow this world of the fathers.

That then is the battle between the evolutionary and the revolutionary forms of emancipation. In many countries, the first is now the official policy at governmental level. Legislation and measures of social reform promote the emancipation of those who formerly suffered from discrimination, and there is a belief that this is not a break in the continuity of our civilization, but a working out of its underlying principles. H. G. Wells, in his *A Short History of the World* (1923), found the meaning of the stage of history of that time in the awareness of the unity of humankind. "For a score of centuries or more the spirit of the great universal religions has been struggling to maintain and extend the idea of a universal human brotherhood.... The idea of human brotherhood struggles now to possess the human soul, just as the idea of Christendom struggled to possess the soul of Europe in the confusion and disorder of the sixth and seventh centuries of the Christian era. The dissemination and triumph of such ideas must be the work of a multitude of devoted and undistinguished missionaries...."[2] Wells believed in persuasion and education through which the true intention of the traditional faiths would be made manifest.

In this connection it is remarkable that Dr Charles Malik, the Rapporteur of the United Nations Commission on Human Rights which drew up the Universal Declaration of Human Rights, interpreted that most remarkable charter of emancipation as an attempt to reaffirm the best traditions of the past over against modern tendencies towards the disintegration of human life. He said of the work of the Commission: "We are trying in effect, knowingly or unknowingly, to go back to the Platonic-Christian tradition which affirms man's original, integral dignity and immortality."[3]

The revolutionary conception of emancipation however denies vehemently that society with its present standards and structures can serve as the framework of emancipated living. It is inherently antagonistic to genuine freedom. The only way out is that of total political, social and cultural revolution.

The most consistent in their position on this subject have been the anarchists. Michael Bakunin gave a clear definition of their aim: "The negation of God and the principles of authority, divine and human, and also of any tutelage by a man over men."[4] Anarchist political movements did not reach a large number of people, but the anarchist spirit penetrated very deeply into modern culture. In the literature of the past hundred years, the idea of total emancipation of the human being through a radical cultural revolution is dominant over traditional values. It is astonishing, as we have said above, that the bourgeois world did not realize, as they applauded the novelists and playwrights who attacked and ridiculed the authority of father figures, that they were helping to undermine their own world.

At the end of the nineteenth and the beginning of the twentieth century, the revolt against father figures became a central theme of discussion among the intelligentsia. Thus, in Schwabing, a suburb of Munich, was to be found the *Kosmische Runde,* a group of men and women of diverse backgrounds, united by the conviction that the time had come to abolish patriarchal authority. They drew their inspiration from the works of Johann Jakob Bachofen, a professor of the University of Basle, who between 1860 and 1885 published a number of books about the ancient Mediterranean civilizations. At first these attracted very little attention. In 1900 however the philosopher Ludwig Klages rediscovered them and shared his enthusiasm for Bachofen's ideas with a number of friends. It may seem strange that the scholarly writings of a professor should have caused so much excitement. The reason was that Bachofen had brought again into the light a forgotten world, the world of ancient religions deeply imbued with the sense of the relationship between the human person and the cosmic forces, religions in which the mother goddess played a central role, which left no room for paternal authority. In Bachofen's view, the key to the history of the classical epoch was the conflict between cultures based on the natural principle and those dominated by the paternal principle. As an active churchman and member of a patrician family, he declared that the victory of the paternal culture, embodied in the Roman Republic and Empire, had been a blessing for humanity, as it had liberated the Western world from the nature-worship of the Orient and had thus enabled it to fulfil its historical mission. In spite of this, Bachofen painted the matriarchal world and the experience of cosmic unity in such glowing colours that he seemed, perhaps unconsciously, to have a deep admiration for it, and the Schwabing group, accepting Bachofen's sharp distinction between the paternal, rational Apollonian world and the maternal, cosmic, Dionysian world, definitely chose the latter.

The Schwabing group had connections with many other contemporary movements. It influenced the *Jugendbewegung,* because Klages became the chief prophet of the new vitalism, teaching, as runs the title of one of his books, that "The Spirit is the Adversary of the Soul". Several members of the group played leading parts in the revolution of the extreme left which broke out in Munich just after the First World War, and one of them, the anarchist Erich Mühsam, was executed when the revolution failed. The group also had close relations with a group in Ascona, Switzerland, which had become a centre of anarchism and cosmic speculations.

Further, there is an interesting link between D. H. Lawrence's philosophy of the life-force and the *Kosmische Runde,* in that Lawrence's wife, Frieda von Richthofen, had been in close touch with the Schwabing group. There is a very strong resemblance between the underlying thesis of Lawrence's works and those of the *Runde.* Both Lawrence and the members of the Schwabing group were 'primitives', who expected a great renewal from a rediscovery of the original cosmic religion. They were 'vitalists' who wanted to cure the ills of civilization by an intensification of life. Bachofen had found in the world of the Etruscans the maternal principle and the Dionysian spontaneity which he contrasted with Roman paternalism with its legalism and discipline. In the same way, Lawrence turned to the Etruscans to find confirmation of his belief in the life-force:

> Evil, what is evil?
> There is only one evil, to deny life
> As Rome denied Etruria
> And mechanical America Montezuma still.

Lawrence was here using the name of the Emperor Montezuma as a symbol of the old American civilizations which he sought to revive in his novel *The Plumed Serpent:*

> For Oh, I know in the dust where we have buried
> The silenced races and all their abominations,
> We have buried so much of the delicate magic of life.[5]

In Lawrence's *The Man who Died,* his anti-Christian bias becomes very clear. According to his wild speculation, Jesus did not die, but escaped from the Cross. He met a priestess of Isis and so discovered the true glory of life. The liberation of human beings is described in these words: "This is the great atonement, the being in touch. The grey sea and the rain, the wet narcissus and the woman I wait for, the invisible Isis and the unseen sun are all in touch, and at one." As Nietzsche did, Lawrence is here proclaiming the victory of Dionysos over the Crucified One.

In the years when the rise of National Socialism was the chief political and ideological issue, this 'vitalist' anarchism lost popularity because it seemed related to the 'Blood and Soil' motive of National Socialist propaganda. Ludwig Klages's ideas, once used by the anarchists, were now employed by the prophets of Germanic racial domination. After the War and the fall of Hitler's Reich, however, there was in the 1950s and even more in the 1960s a great renaissance of anarchism among the intellectuals. Its most successful advocate was Herbert Marcuse. His *Eros and Civilization,* published in 1955, is one great plea for the liberation of the life instincts from the repression imposed by our civilization. He made full use of Freud's analysis of the development of civilized society. This begins with a 'primal father' who is 'the archetype of domination' amd who "initiates the chain reaction of enslavement, rebellion and reinforced domination which marks the history of civilization."[6] Domination is described in these words: "The patriarch, father and tyrant in one, unites sex and order, pleasure and reality; he evokes love and hatred; he guarantees the biological and sociological basis on which the history of mankind depends." In another passage he writes: "As the father is multiplied, supplemented and replaced by the authorities of society, as prohibitions and inhibitions spread, so do the aggressive impulse and its objects."

Freud said that our civilization was generally speaking founded on the suppression of instincts. Now Freud was not a revolutionary. He saw society as 'static' and believed that the repressive basis of civilization could not be changed in any way. At this point, Marcuse parts company with him and turns to Nietzsche with his 'eternal Yes of Being' *(Ewiges Ja des Seins)*. Nietzsche's conception of liberation was that mankind must come to associate bad conscience not with the affirmation but with the denial of the life instincts, not with rebellion but with the acceptance of repressive ideals. By thus combining Freud and Nietzsche, Marcuse accumulated an impressive amount of dynamite for the undermining of the established order. For if Freud was right in stating that the life instincts are repressed by 'fathers' and all that they represent, and if Nietzsche is right in believing that the one and only norm of human existence must be that of 'being-as-an-end-in-itself', then the obvious task of the human being, and particularly of the young, is to revolt against paternalist domination. *Eros and Civilization* did not describe in any detail the nature of the revolution which Marcuse had in mind. In 1966, however, he wrote a new preface in which he introduced the Marxist doctrine of revolution and combined the "revolt against the false fathers, teachers and heroes" with "solidarity with the wretched of the earth." The preface ended with an appeal to youth: "By nature, the young are in the forefront of those who live and fight for Eros against Death, and against a civilization which tries to shorten the 'detour to death' while controlling the means for lengthening the detour." The appeal from his point of view could not have been timed more efficiently. It came just at the right moment to provide ammunition for the great revolt of youth in 1968.

13. How far will emancipation go?

It must now be asked whether emancipation is a process which will continue until the end of time, or whether it is characteristic of certain periods of history, particularly our own. Does it follow a straight line, a spiral or the swinging of a pendulum? These difficult questions can be answered adequately only in the setting of the theology and philosophy of history. As emancipation from paternalism is part of a wider movement, I must at least indicate briefly the historical perspective in which I see it.

In 1900, Lord Rosebery, a former Liberal Prime Minister of the United Kingdom, said that the nineteenth century had been "an Era of Emancipation, considerable though not complete."[1] This was true in more senses than one, because it was in that century that emancipation ceased to be the dream of a few philosophers and became the ideal of large masses of people. It was also then that the idea of emancipation as a continuing process became a leading tendency in the philosophy of history. Reinhold Niebuhr wrote: "Though there are minor dissonances, the whole chorus of modern culture learned to sing the new song of hope in remarkable harmony. The redemption of mankind, by whatever means, was assured for the future. It was, in fact, assured by the future."[2] The marvellous discoveries made by scientists, the progress of democracy, the new self-awareness of the working class, the liberation movements in various countries, all seemed to show that men were making enormous strides towards freedom. Optimism about progress was more than a popular faith. It was propagated in leading intellectual circles. Thus Alexis de Tocqueville, the sober-minded interpreter of American democracy, wrote in 1839 that the emerging of conditions of equality was the work of Providence, universal and enduring. "It defeated every attempt at resistance, and to try to stop it amounted to a struggle against God himself."[3]

Niebuhr had mentioned 'minor dissonances'. They were perhaps minor in that they represented the point of view of isolated individuals, but they were not of minor importance, when one considers the quality of the people who spoke thus in warning tones.

In 1867, Thomas Carlyle made a sharp attack on the general enthusiasm for emancipation. He spoke sarcastically of the "general repeal of old regulations, fetters and restrictions which had become unpleasant", a development which was welcomed "with loud shouting from the multitude, as strap after strap is cut: glory, glory, another strap is gone", so that "the Devil is become an emancipated gentleman."[4] Jacob Burckhardt, the great Swiss historian, expressed his doubts in less aggressive tones. He was shocked by the lack of respect for the great cultural traditions shown by the classes which were rising, and when he saw signs of the revolutionary movements which culminated in 1848, he left for Italy, in order to live amid the great cultural treasures of the past. In 1873, he wrote that the world was moving not towards a liberal democracy but towards a tyrannical state, and foretold that authoritarianism rather than freedom would be the characteristic of the twentieth century.[5] Similarly, in his famous lectures on world history he said: "The end of the story is that somewhere the inequality of men will again be honoured."[6]

There were also some who had at first embraced the doctrine of salvation by science, but who, as time went on, realized that it was not fulfilling its apparent promise. In 1847-1848, Ernest Renan wrote a book on the future of science[7] in which he spoke, in the emotional tones of a recent convert, of the redemptive role which science was destined to play. It would replace religion and would show that the true standard was not any transcendental truth, but that offered by the human being. Thus Renan began by seeing the process of emancipation as a continuous ascent towards the light, but when he published this book many years later, in 1890, he confessed his deep concern over the impossibility of creating a 'catechism' for modern man. The old Christian catechism was no longer relevant but science had not produced a new truth by which men and women could live. He ended by asking *De quoi vivra-t-on après nous?* — by what would coming generations live?

Another more recent example of a radical change of mind about human progress and emancipation is that which overtook

H. G. Wells. In his *A Short History of the World,* written in the optimistic early 1920s, when the slogan 'no more war' was on many lips and people believed in internationalism, he was the prophet of unlimited progress and emancipation. "Can we doubt that presently our race will more than realize our boldest imaginations, that it will achieve unity and peace, that it will live, the children of our blood and lives will live, in a world made more splendid and lovely than any place or garden that we know, going on from strength to strength in an ever widening circle of adventure and achievement?"[8] Shortly before his death in 1946, however, he wrote: "Hitherto events have been held together by a certain logical consistency as the heavenly bodies have been held together by the golden cord of gravitation. Now it is as if the cord had vanished and everything is driven anyhow, anywhere, at a steadily increasing velocity.... The writer is convinced that there is no way out, or through the impasse. It is the end."[9]

The main reason for the disillusionment of these men was the fact that what Martin Buber had called, in a title to one of his books, *Paths to Utopia,* were turning out to be blind alleys. Many had believed in the Utopia in which science was to make men and women the master of their destiny. Comte's description of the three ages of the world, the theological, the metaphysical and the scientific, had found wide acceptance. Science was to replace religion as the basis of culture, giving it meaning and ethical norms. Before long it would be possible through biology, psychology and sociology to develop a new type of the human being.

Spiritual adventurers like Dostoevsky and Nietzsche had already ridiculed this naive rationalism, but the prestige of science remained high until the twentieth century, when it became more and more obvious that while scientists were very successful in dealing with natural matter, they were unable to solve the problems of people's attitude to nature and to their fellows. The tremendous contrast between the great technocratic victories, such as the discovery of atomic energy and the achievement of space travel and defeat in the fields of pollution of the oceans, deterioration of the environment and failure to limit atomic armaments created grave doubt as to whether the ultimate impact of science on human life would be beneficial.

The world was at the mercy of the technocratic imperative — "What can be done must be done" — which meant that the human being was the victim of inventions and techniques resulting from a scientific approach which had no criteria or standards, for most scientists declared that values and norms of action were not their concern.

There were many who had hoped that emancipation from the patriarchal world would lead to a socio-political Utopia. Once liberated from the traditional paternalistic and oppressive forces which had imprisoned them, people would at last be able to build a society based on freedom and justice. The achievement of liberty is indeed a great victory but, as Reinhold Niebuhr reminds us: "Every new freedom represented a new peril as well as a new promise."[10] A society of emancipated men and women "also created atomic individuals, freed from the disciplines of the older organic communities" who were "lost in the mass and became the prey of demagogues."

In other words, the struggle for freedom was pointless unless it were accompanied by new forms of community. The only new structures which offered themselves were various types of socialism, communism and anarchism. All these systems promised that the human person would be enabled to live in fellowship and fraternal collaboration and would enjoy true freedom. But were these promises fulfilled?

Martin Buber, in a dispassionate analysis of the subject, came to the conclusion that they were not. None of them has in fact given people the structure of a common life in which they were united on a voluntary basis to perform common tasks, without constraint or interference from the state.

It is the tragedy of Marxism that, instead of developing a decentralized society, as had been the intention, it led to the greatest possible centralization. The socialist movement had hoped to lead to "the voluntary combination of people into small independent units of communal life and work and the voluntary combination of those into a community of communities".[11] The USSR however became "an immense, utterly centralized complex of state production centres and state distribution centres, a mechanism of bureaucratically run institutes for production and consumption.... As for spontaneity, free association, there is no longer any room for them whatever." A bureaucratic and centralized society inevitably becomes tyrannical and that was not the society of which the critics of capitalism had dreamed. For a time it looked as if China, or perhaps Cuba, might fulfil the promise but in the field of international affairs these countries proved to be no different from the rest. The disappointment which this caused to many found some partial expression in the creation by groups or individuals or communes of one kind or another, in the hope that out of such small, experimental beginnings, a new order might arise.

The idea of a Utopia based on culture also has disappointed its adherents. It had been hoped that it would be possible to develop a counter-culture to set over against the cold, mechanical, rationalistic world of technocracy; a counter-culture which would be Dionysian rather than Apollonian. One of its aims would be to restore unity between the human being and nature, to stop the shameful exploitation of natural resources and to express faith in the dynamic life-force. As the French writer, Roger Garaudy, put it: "The only god which they (the young) can conceive of and live with, after Marx, Nietzsche and Freud, in an epoch in which substance is becoming, mass is energy, being is relating, is the creative force at the heart of all things. God is there where something new is coming to birth in artistic creation, a scientific discovery, a love or a revolution."[12] So the disciples of this counter-culture began to move, to dance, to travel, to run as fast as possible in all directions. But did they find what they were seeking? The "new, eclective religious revival" is described by Theodore Roszak as a syncretism resembling "nothing so much as the cultic hothouse of the Hellenistic period with every manner of mystery and fakery, ritual and rite, intermingled with marvellous indiscrimination."[13] The flight from traditional fathers has often ended in submission to a new father, a guru or autocratic sect-leader. The question arises whether it is possible to create any culture on the basis of pure vitalism. The Greeks knew that it was not enough to live by Dionysos. The shrine at Delphi was dedicated both to Apollo and Dionysos. A purely Dionysian culture is inconceivable, because the very meaning of culture is that form is given to the vital forces. There can be no creation without discipline.

The counter-culture therefore remained sterile. It did not produce the art, the thought, the community which had been expected. It was in many ways a necessary corrective to traditional culture, but it was not an alternative to it.

The short-coming common to all these expressions of dissatisfaction with life is that in all of these 'new worlds', there is no generally accepted system of values and convictions, no agreement as to the meaning of life, which is necessary to make a coherent society with a purpose which its members can share. The struggle for emancipation has shown the depth of the human desire for freedom but has failed to satisfy the human wish for participation in a larger whole which would give deeper significance to the life of each individual. Auguste Comte understood this, and elaborated a new "religion of humanity" destined to perform the social and cultural function fulfilled in the Middle Ages by the great conception of one unified Christendom. His mistake was that he believed a new religion could be created at a desk. The German philosopher, Rudolf Eucken, wrote in 1904: "We become increasingly aware that all external triumphs do not prevent an inner decline.... For in spite of all talk about unity and equality, humanity has less and less cohesion; we lack common ideas and convictions which can unite and strengthen us."[14]

During the Munich crisis of 1938, Dr J. H. Oldham, one of the pioneers, as we have seen, of the ecumenical movement, wrote a letter to *The Times* in which he said: "The banal truth is that the spiritual foundations of Western civilization have been undermined. The systems which are in the ascendant on the Continent may be regarded from one point of view as convulsive attempts to arrest the process of disintegration. What clear alternative have we in this country?" Oldham succeeded in bringing together a number of men who could help in answering that question, and I was invited to attend some of their meetings. It was a remarkable group, including Arnold Toynbee, Middleton Murry, Donald McKinnon and T. S. Eliot among others. Out of these meetings emerged, as one result, T. S. Eliot's *Idea of a Christian Society*. The poet described modern Western culture as a culture of liberalism. Liberalism had performed a useful function, but it was fundamentally a negative function. "It is a movement not so much defined by its end as by its starting point; away from, rather than towards something definite."[15] Eliot thus pleaded for a positive cultural concept and for a rediscovery of the idea of a Christian society.

Such warnings and challenges were much discussed during the Second World War and in the years immediately following it. Later, however, the vision of a spiritual reintegration of society seemed to have become far removed from reality. In considering culture, the new key word was 'pluralism'. Many, myself included, emphasized the great advantages of a pluralistic culture, in which all ideologies and philosophies would have the opportunity to express themselves. It was, however, not sufficiently understood that a consistent pluralism leads to a situation in which there is no longer one culture but a great number of diverse cultures which have no longer a common language, a common set of values or a common frame of reference. Emancipation leads to pluralism, but pluralism leads to chaos unless it is accompanied by a vital common faith which provides explanations regarding human destiny and the meaning of human life. In particular, legislators and judges are unable to operate on the basis of a full-fledged pluralism.

If the outcome of emancipation has proved so disappointing, must it not be concluded that it would be better to stop the whole process? One answer to this question is that attempts to resist emancipation have to all intents and purposes resulted in failure. To take illustrations from the nineteenth and twentieth centuries, the first was the resistance on a large scale made by the members of the Holy Alliance, with Metternich as the key figure. His success in retarding emancipation from the Congress of Vienna until the revolutions of 1848 was an astounding achievement, but he won all his battles except the last. His collaborator, Friedrich Gentz, had had no illusions on the subject. He said: "I was always aware that the spirit of the times *(Zeitgeist)* would in the long run prove more powerful .... and that neither diplomatic power nor violence can arrest the wheels of the world."[16]

Further unsuccessful resistance to movements of emancipation was that offered by Pope Pius IX. He was not the only churchman, nor was his the only church, to resist what were called 'modern ideas'. In the Netherlands, the Anti-revolutionary Party led by Groen van Prinsterer and Abraham Kuyper also fought against the ideology introduced by the French Revolution. Pope Pius IX however went further than any other church leader. In 1864, he issued an Encyclical to which was annexed a 'Syllabus of Errors', naming 80 of these, many of which had already been condemned in previous papal statements. The Syllabus has been called a declaration of war against modern culture. That this is no exaggeration is shown by the following paragraph: "If anyone says that the Roman Pontiff can, and ought to, reconcile himself to, and agree with, progress, liberalism and modern civilization, let him be anathema."[17] The document went on to state that modern civilization was characterized by the emancipation of the layman and by the 'laicization' of society, and this meant the undermining of all authority. In the Encyclical *Pascendi Gregis* of 1907, Pope Pius X wrote that one of the errors of modernists was that they believed the force of progress to reside in individual consciences. The Pope asked: "Do you not see here, venerable brethren, the pernicious doctrine which makes the laity in the Church a factor of progress?" When my grandfather, an ardent Freemason, read these lines, he pencilled two exclamation marks in the margin.

About a hundred years after the publication of the Syllabus, the Second Vatican Council discussed the role of "The Church in the Modern World". The outcome was the Constitution *Gaudium et Spes,* to which we have referred above and which can be described as an olive branch offered to modern culture. The Council looked critically at the contemporary world, but it spoke with appreciation of some of that world's main tendencies. As an illustration of the change of direction, one of the Council fathers, the Indian Archibshop D'Souza, said in his address: "The first part of our text speaks of the dignity of man, of responsibility and the freedom of conscience. A declaration of the rights of men and of citizens was already formulated by the American and French Revolutions. Only 176 years later does the Church recognize religious freedom and the rights of pluralistic society, after having rejected them on many occasions."[18] Instead of deploring the coming of age of humanity, the Church now showed understanding for this great historical fact.

The third great attempt to arrest the forces of emancipation is so well-known and recent that there is no need to discuss it at length. Fascism and National Socialism made it their openly proclaimed objective to reverse the trends of European history. On Freedom, Hitler said: "If you leave men their individual freedom, they behave like apes." With regard to democracy, he said: "There must be unconditional authority from the top downwards, and absolute responsibility towards superiors." His system differed from democracies which allow people to be responsible to those who are below them — and which represented, in his view, "a crazy turning upside down of all human organization."[19] On the relation between the leader and the people, the dictator showed himself to be a modern version of the ancient authoritarian *pater*

familias, for he said: "The reason why the mass of the people sub-
mits willingly to leadership is that it has a feminine disposition."
He added that, while women might cause trouble, at the bottom of
their hearts they did not want to take the lead in the life of a
couple. In the same way, the people wanted leadership from
leaders. Thus National Socialists and Fascists were convinced that
they had succeeded in giving a completely new orientation to
European history. The age of emancipation was over, and as
Goebbels said, 1789, the date of the outbreak of the French Revolution, could now be struck from the calendar. As it turned out, the
National Socialist revolution succeeded in arresting the march
towards emancipation only for the short period of twelve years.

In these twelve years, many of us who were involved in the
struggle against National Socialism became more keenly aware of
the priceless value of our heritage of spiritual, intellectual and religious freedom. Across national, social and confessional frontiers,
those who resisted tyranny became brothers. During the war, Dietrich Bonhoeffer and I belonged to nations which were in grim
conflict with each other, but we were deeply united in one
common effort to find a strong foundation for a new era of
freedom.[20] In 1944, representatives of a number of European
resistance movements met in 'a European city'. In fact, they met in
my home in Geneva and, in their Declaration, they referred to a
new consciousness of European solidarity, born out of the sacrifices and suffering of the war years.

They proposed the creation of a European Federation of
Nations which would be based on the recognition of human rights,
both political and economic, on free personal development and
the normal functioning of democratic institutions.[21] Thus the
lessons we learned from Hitler were the opposite of those he had
wished to teach us.

Does this then mean that the march of people towards emancipation is irresistible and will go on for ever? This difficult question
I must answer under two points. In the first place, it must be remembered that, in the process of emancipation which I have
described, many groups of people have been neglected, in the
sense that their emancipation has not yet begun or is at an early
stage. It now seems inevitable that such groups will demand their
rights, inspired by the example of those who have already reached
a new stage of freedom. This applies to many situations in the

third world where large sections of the population have not yet or only recently been touched by modern ideas of human rights. It applies also to the second world, in so far as communist regimes interpret human rights mainly if not entirely as economic rights, and do not permit the individual that self-expression, including the right to express criticism and dissent, which mature men and women demand, thus creating conditions in which the pressure for emancipation steadily increases. Also in the first world of the West, there are those who have been forgotten or who are late-comers in the process, and who will certainly strive to catch up. There are groups of women, racial groups, foreign workers and others who will not rest until they feel themselves to be on an equal footing with their fellow-citizens.

Secondly, I believe that history is "the story of man's developing freedom",[22] and that emancipation is therefore a process which will continue. It is not however a process which will lead automatically to a state of perfect freedom. The theory of a process of cosmic evolution of this kind has been worked out by the French philosopher Teilhard de Chardin. Following in his footsteps, Peter Berglar has written a most stimulating book in which he describes the meaning of such an evolution as the transformation of the world of the fathers into the world of the brothers, who accept one another as equals.[23] But this view of history underestimates the negative aspects of freedom. As we have seen, emancipation can have highly beneficial results for individuals and human relations, but the increase in freedom brings with it new perils. People can abuse freedom to such an extent that it becomes a destructive force in their lives and in society. History teaches us not only that people have sought greater freedom, but also that they have allowed this freedom to become corrupted, so that it leads to ego-centricity, self-assertion and disintegration. There has never been certainty that before the end of time a fully fraternal world will come about.

Emancipation therefore has its limits and whether or not some act of emancipation leads to a serious disintegration of the society in which it takes place, that society, in order to ensure its own survival, is likely to react by imposing measures to restrict any further advance towards freedom. Those who speak of total emancipation must therefore ask themselves whether any society based on total human freedom would have sufficient order and cohesion to operate and to prove durable. Emancipation is not an end in itself, but must be considered in relation to the whole calling of humanity. It has to find its proper place in a conception of the human person and of history which can answer the question "Emancipation for what?"

14. Divine fatherhood without paternalism

We must now turn to the central problem of our investigation and decide whether there is a fundamental incompatibility between maturity and the service of God the Father whom Jesus proclaims and reveals. Does the God of the Bible seek to arrest the emancipation of people and, if so, must twentieth century men and women abandon this God, if they wish to stand on their own feet? Is the biblical God so much a part of ancient, antiquated, patriarchal society that he cannot speak to us today?

To answer these questions we must concentrate entirely on the interpretation which Jesus himself gives of the fatherhood of God. Avoiding distraction from all the associations which have become attached to the concept of fatherhood from Jesus' time to our own, we must seek to hear again the 'Good News', the original message about God the Father which Jesus brought to us, and brings to us still.

Our starting point must be the first indication which Jesus gave concerning his calling. When Mary and Joseph found the boy in the Temple and asked him why he had stayed behind, he answered in astonishment: "Do you not know that I must be in my Father's house?"[1] His unique relationship with God — the Father who directed and guided him — was the unshakable foundation of Jesus' life. It was not a philosophical conviction regarding the fatherhood of God, nor was there in it any speculation about God's paternal qualities. It was his constant awareness of the presence of a loving father who had entrusted his son with a message and a mission to humankind. This finds its clearest expression in the word 'Abba' — the Aramaic word used by a child when addressing its father — which Jesus employs when speaking to

God. We find it in his prayer in Gethsemane, as given in the Gospel according to St Mark.[2] The fact that the evangelist here introduced the Aramaic word in addition to the Greek word *pater* surely indicates that, in describing this moment of crisis, he wanted to use the word which Jesus himself had used. Again, in Romans 8: 14-17 and in Galatians 4: 6-7, 'Abba' is the cry which characterizes the spirit of sonship, because it was thus that Jesus called upon his Father. Joachim Jeremias has written: "It was an everyday word used within the family which nobody would have dared to use in speaking to God. Jesus has dared this. He speaks to his heavenly Father with such confidence, in such a childlike and intimate manner as a small child to its father."[3]

Jesus' communication with his Father has the nature of a close personal relationship based on complete confidence. All that he says and does is a manifestation of the Father's gracious will. "The Abba experience", says Edward Schillebeeckx "would appear to be the source of the peculiar nature of Jesus' message and conduct, which, without this religious experience, or apart from it, lose the distinctive meaning and content actually conferred on them by Jesus."[4]

Jesus brings to all men and women an invitation to become his partners in this life with the Father. He offers us a share in that communion, and this is what is meant by "becoming as little children."[5] In the interpretation of Joachim Jeremias, "If you do not learn to say 'Abba', you will not be able to enter into the Kingdom of God."[6]

In a much discussed passage in St Matthew 11 (25-27) and St Luke 10 (21-22), Jesus thanks his Father because he has hidden 'these things' from the wise and understanding and revealed them to babes. He says: "All things have been delivererd to me by the Father, and no one knows the Father except the Son and anyone to whom the Son chooses to reveal him." Many scholars consider the phrasing of this last verse so typically Greek that they doubt whether Jesus actually used these words. But, as Schillebeeckx says: "In essence at any rate, Matt. 11: 27 may be called an authentic Jesus-saying,"[7] for it puts in a nutshell all that the New Testament proclaims, namely that it is because of the coming of Jesus that we can enter into communion with God and discover the nature of his fatherhood. We owe it to Jesus that we can pray 'Our Father', not only because he taught us the prayer, but also because he invites us to join the family of his Father. "To say the Lord's prayer is to enter into the filial consciousness of Jesus in his relation to God."[8] Since we received our knowledge of God's fatherhood from Jesus, we must accept his interpretation, and no other, concerning the nature of that fatherhood.

The setting of the life and teaching of Jesus is of course the Jewish society of his time, with its patriarchal ethos and social structure. The householder of the parables was the head of a large family, which included not only his own wife and children, but also his servants and their children. He had complete control over all members of this extended family, even over his grown-up sons, for they continued to live in their father's house.

Typically patriarchal also was the attitude of the contemporaries of Jesus to women. Women and children could be sold to pay a debt. Married men had the right to divorce their wives by unilateral decision.[9] Men were not to talk to women in the street, in particular not teachers of the Law, for it was believed that women could not understand the true meaning of what was taught.[10]

The attitude of Jesus to this patriarchal world was one of astonishing freedom. He did not reject patriarchal standards, but confirmed their validity as a means of bringing order into the life of society. On the other hand, he did not consider them as a sufficient or definitive guide to human conduct. He did not put himself above the Law, but he showed that the work of God among people must come before the Law. Human beings must seek first the Kingdom of God, and their loyalty to it came before any loyalty to human authority.

We have referred already to the journey made by the young Jesus with his parents to Jerusalem, a visit made in accordance with the old tradition. When on the way home the boy is missed, he is found in the Temple, among the teachers. In one sense he had disobeyed his parents, but his actions were in obedience to his Father in Heaven, and further, as Karl Barth reminds us, he had simply remained "at the source to which his parents themselves had brought him."[11] The evangelist went on to show that this event did not mean that Jesus had rejected the old commandments, for, as he wrote: "He went down with them and came to Nazareth, and was obedient to them."[12]

At first sight there appears to be a strong contradiction between the emphasis put by Jesus on the commandment to honour one's father and one's mother[13] and his severe words "Who are my mother and my brothers...?"[14]

This scene illustrates again the question of priority in loyalties. In the passage in the Gospel of St Mark[15], we read that when the family of Jesus came to him, "a crowd was sitting about him." In other words, he was at that moment working for and with his Father, and was making it clear that the *familia dei* takes precedence over the natural family. "Whoever does the will of God is my brother, and sister, and mother."[16]

This is confirmed by the passage about discipleship in the Gospel of St Luke 14, verse 26, which is the strongest expression of the priority of the commitment to the Kingdom to be found in the New Testament: "If anyone comes to me and does not hate his own father and mother and wife and children and brothers and sisters, yes, and even his own life, he cannot be my disciple." The Aramaic word here translated as 'hate' actually means "to give second place in one's affections", as can be seen from St Matthew 10, verse 37, which reads "He who loves father or mother more than me is not worthy of me..." *Sub specie aeternitatis* family ties have no absolute validity.

In the same way, Jesus shows that the relationship of a disciple to his rabbi or human teacher is also relative: "And call no man your father on earth, for you have one Father, who is in heaven."[17] No one must become so dependent on human authority that he or she cannot listen to the Father.

The freedom with which Jesus treated patriarchal customs was also clear in his attitude to women. It was very unusual in his times that women should be included in the group of his disciples and friends.[18] Even more remarkable was the fact that Jesus was as willing to teach women as to teach men.[19] Here again, God's concern for human beings takes precedence over all convention. Similarly, in the discussion on divorce, Jesus went as far as to question the authority of the Mosaic Law as expressed in the Book of Deuteronomy,[20] by which a man could make a one-sided decision to put his wife away. Jesus made it clear that women were as much the object of God's care as men. The original intention of marriage was that man and woman should become one.[21] No man, no law or custom should put asunder what God joined together. Thus, far from abolishing the commandments given by God to the children of Israel, Jesus was giving them 'Messianic intensification'[22], and revealing their true intention. When the authority of human tradition, 'the tradition of the elders' as the Gospel according to St Mark puts it,[23] seeks to compromise with that intention, Jesus does not recognize that authority.

It is in his teaching about the nature of God that Jesus' freedom from patriarchalism is most clearly seen. An excellent example is the parable of the labourers in the vineyard.[24] The owner is the typical master whose will is sovereign law for his household. "Am I not allowed to do what I choose with what belongs to me?"[25] Those listening to Jesus would expect that the master was either just, and paid what was due to the labourers, or unjust, so that he gave them less than they had earned. It was a totally new idea to them that a master might pay the same to those who had worked for an hour as to those who had laboured the whole day. But the parable was designed to show that, although God's power might be compared to that of a patriarchal master, it was by no means certain that he would act as such a master would. God had a surprising way of breaking through all human calculations, and the listeners were not to think of him in terms of the social relationships familiar to them but as a Father whose generous love embraced all his children, and especially those who needed it most.

That God the Father transcends the limits of patriarchalism is even more clearly expressed in the parable of the prodigal son, which, according to Joachim Jeremias, should really be called the Parable of the Father's Love. The traditional belief was that it was the duty of sons to remain in their father's house under his control, as did the elder son, who said: "Lo, these many years I have served you, and I never disobeyed your command."[26] By these standards, the departure of the younger son was an act of rebellion and the father could, and perhaps even should, have refused to permit it. The law as set forth in the Book of Deuteronomy prescribed that a stubborn and rebellious son should be brought to the elders of the city to be stoned to death.[27] The father in the parable however permitted his son to take his own decision. He gave him his share of the property and allowed him to go, not through weakness or lack of authority, but because he was unwilling to force his son to stay at home. He wanted him to come to a free decision about their relationship and, in his hopeful and patient love, he was willing to wait. And he did not wait in vain. The son returned, and was greeted, not with a rebuke, but with that embrace depicted by Rembrandt in an unforgettable painting which makes the Hermitage Gallery in Leningrad a place of powerful witness to the grace of God.

The elder son had thought of his rights in legal terms. He felt it unjust that his faithful service was unrecognized, while a feast was prepared for his irresponsible brother. As G. B. Caird has put it in his commentary on St Luke, "the obedience he is so proud of has been slavish and mercenary, never filial", and his father has to show him why he has treated his younger son with more than simple justice: "This your brother was dead, and is alive; he was lost, and is found."

In the Gospel according to St John, a clear distinction is made between the relationship of a master to a servant, and that of a father to a son. "The slave does not continue in the house for ever; the son continues for ever. So if the son makes you free, you will be free indeed."[28] The hierarchical terminology used in the patriarchal world is out of date. "No longer do I call you servants, for the servant does not know what his master is doing, but I have called you friends, for all that I have heard from my Father I have made known to you."[29]

The most profound interpretation of the meaning of God's fatherhood is found in the witness of the New Testament concerning the relation between God and Jesus as the Son of God. It is through the life of the Son that we come to know the Father. The Son of God in the person of Jesus is totally different from others to whom this title had been given in the surrounding Hellenistic world. Emperors and men who claimed divine powers had been so called.

To Jesus, sonship meant not power but obedience and his life among men was an overwhelming demonstration of freely accepted humiliation. The contrast between these two conceptions of sonship was underlined at the very start of his ministry. The tempter in the wilderness said to him: "If you are the Son of God, command these stones to become loaves of bread;"[30] and again, "If you are the Son of God, throw yourself down."[31] But Jesus knew that to perform miracles only to prove his power was not God's way. "The Kingdom of God is not coming with signs to be observed."[32] He knew that God did not give external proofs of his power. The Father's way with his children may at first sight seem to be a way of weakness, but it leads to ultimate victory.

We find the same insight in Jesus' spontaneous exclamation: "I thank thee, Father, Lord of heaven and earth, that thou hast hidden these things from the wise and understanding and revealed them to babes."[33] He is grateful that the good news is not information available without effort, because he wishes people not simply to learn about his love but to be transformed by it as can happen only if they turn to him with confidence and expectation, as do little children. It is because the presence of the Father is to be discovered that men and women can decide for faith and for personal communion with him.

In his life, the Son showed that the Father was not like earthly rulers who 'lord it' over their people.[34] Though he knows that "the Father has given all things into his hands", he washes the feet of his disciples.[35] John says: "For God so loved the world that he gave his only Son"[36] — gave him to humanity, and in doing so, delivered him up to die. Paul repeats this idea when he says that God "did not spare his own Son, but gave him up for us all."[37] God was therefore willing to accept defeat so that, through it, he might bring men and women to realize his fatherly love.

All the themes of the Son's humiliation, his obedience, his acceptance of the status of a servant, his willingness to sacrifice himself and the ultimate victory of the glory of the Father are brought together in the doxological hymn in the Epistle to the Philippians.[38] Jesus Christ, the Son, who was "in the form of God" and who lived the divine life, accepted a double humiliation in that he not only identified himself with people, but even with the most powerless among them. His resurrection, his ultimate victory, is indissolubly linked with his crucifixion. And his followers must not expect to share in his victory if they forget that he "reigns from the Cross".

As the Dutch theologian Hendrik Berkhof has written, "God has decided to lose power in order to give communion. His defencelessness is his gracious unwillingness to be omnipotent without us and against us."[39] Berkhof calls this "the defenceless superiority of God" and to this helpful formula, I would add only, "and his hidden presence."

It is strange that this fundamental aspect of God's work has been so often neglected or forgotten in the history of the church.

This is surely due to the deep-rooted desire of people for a success story rather than a story of humiliation. For example, the entry of Jesus into Jerusalem is generally referred to as 'the triumphal entry', though the Gospels present it as the anti-triumphal arrival of the humble king of the prophet Zechariah,[40] a king who does not come in victory.

On the other hand, there have been a number of witnesses to the defencelessness of Jesus and the hidden character of his Sonship. Luther often stressed that all things which were to be believed had to be hidden to leave room for faith. Luther believed that: "The true God is not in fact the omnipotent monarch whose glory the religious attempt to reflect, but One who divests himself of power, who hides himself under the opposite of what the world recognize as omnipotence."[41] In a letter to Mlle de Roannez, Pascal wrote that God "remained hidden from us under the veil of nature until the Incarnation, and when he had to appear, he hid himself even further under his humanity." Kierkegaard wrote in his *Einübung im Christentum* of the 'incognito' of Christ, adding that the indirect communication received in this way puts before the human person the choice of accepting it by faith or rejecting it. Dostoevsky, in the story of the Grand Inquisitor, sought to elucidate why Jesus had not used his power to give us indubitable proof of his divinity. "Thou didst not come down from the Cross when they shouted to Thee, mocking and reviling Thee, 'Come down from the cross and we will believe that Thou art He'. Thou didst not come down, for again Thou wouldst not enslave man by a miracle and didst crave faith given freely."[42] Dietrich Bonhoeffer wrote from his prison cell: "The Bible directs man to God's powerlessness and suffering; only the suffering God can help."[43]

Once again we must consider whether the God whom Jesus proclaimed and revealed is a paternalistic God. Paternalism is resistance to the process of emancipation, the process of coming of age. The typical paternalist does not want his child or pupil to stand on his or her own feet and to assume full responsibility for his or her own life. We have seen, however, that according to the teaching of Jesus, and especially in the light of the revelation given in his life and death, God gives people room to live in freedom and wants them to respond to him spontaneously and not by constraint.

Paternalism is a situation in which the father and the sons are competing with one another in a struggle for power. Jesus tells us, however, that God is in no sense our competitor. "When I call upon God as the Father, I acknowledge that I receive my existence from another, but at the same time I identify myself with him as a son and as a human being called to work with others for the Kingdom."[44]

Paternalism is further the abuse of a father's power, the imposition of the external authority of a law which is to be obeyed because the father says so. The authority of Jesus speaks to the hearts of men and women. He does not manipulate them, but treats every human being as a 'Thou' and not as an 'It'.

Paternalistic men treat women as second-rate beings who are expected to remain under the guardianship of their husbands or fathers, without making their own specific contribution to the spiritual and intellectual life of humanity. In the life and teaching of Jesus, however, there is no such discrimination and he called women to enter the Kingdom exactly as he called men.

The paternal tradition is used to immobilize moral life and tolerates no new insight into God's will. Jesus opens the doors to a living relationship with God in which men and women constantly make new discoveries. Paternalism is basically triumphalist, and paternalists think in terms of power, hierarchy and domination. But at the heart of the gospel is a Cross on which a suffering servant died.

Hans Küng makes this point clearly when he writes: "This Father God is nothing like the God feared by Marx, Nietzsche and Freud, terrifying men from childhood onward into feelings of anxiety and guilt, constantly moralizingly pursuing him: a God who is in fact only the projection of instilled fears, of human domination, lust for power, arrogance and vindictiveness."[45]

The revolt against the Father-God is therefore to a very considerable extent a revolt against a caricature of the true God whom we come to know through Jesus. The caricature is sadly not simply a fabrication of the enemies of Christianity, but owes many of its features to the blindness of Christians themselves. To rid ourselves of this caricature is to get rid of a foolishness of human origin and leaves us face to face with the true, divine foolishness of the gospel which shames the wise.

15. The motherhood of God

In speaking of the fatherhood of God, we must also face the question raised in recent years by a number of theologians as to whether we must not also consider the motherhood of God. In a working paper of the World Council of Churches,[1] we read: "The problem of language and imagery about God has emerged in fresh ways in the contemporary world... Both generic language and the conventional use of male and female language in speaking about God and the Church stand in the way of a Christian community in which all can participate fully." One of the questions which this working paper proposes for study is: "As women's consciousness changes, the call for new language in speaking of God becomes urgent. Although it is understood that God transcends all male and female characteristics, does your language reflect this correctly? Or does your language describe God predominantly in male terms and categories?"

There are many men and not a few women who dismiss this question with irritation or even indignation, but it has clearly become a real problem for the growing number of women who long for a church and society in which men and women may feel equally at home. Christians must therefore ask themselves whether the revelation of God received from the Bible permits us to speak of the motherhood of God.

In the Old Testament there is only one text in which God is quite explicitly described as a motherly God. In Isaiah 66: 13 we read: "As one whom his mother comforts, so I will comfort you." There are however a number of other texts in which the maternal quality of God's love and mercy is described, though in a more indirect way. Thus we find in Isaiah 49: 15: "Can a woman forget her suckling child that she should have no compassion on the son of her womb?" There is another verse which is often translated as if it did not refer to motherhood, but which in fact contains one of the finest descriptions of this quality to be found in the Old Testament. George Adam Smith, the well-known Scottish theologian, gave this liberal translation of Isaiah 31: 5: "As little mother-birds hovering so will Jehovah of hosts protect Jerusalem." The image is that of a mother bird protecting her young from imminent attack. It is interesting to note that George Adam Smith, writing at the end of the last century before feminism had become a force, interpreted this verse as a strong affirmation of the motherhood of God. He referred to a "motherhood of pity in the breast of God" and said that, since all fullness dwells in God himself, "not only may we rejoice in that pity and wise provision for our wants, in that pardon and generosity which we associate with the name of father, but also in the wakefulness, the patience, the love, lovelier with fear, which makes a mother's heart so dear and indispensable." When George Adam Smith used the term 'motherhood of God', he put it in inverted commas. I take it that he did not want to present his reflections on this subject as a new dogma, but rather as a correction and completion of our thinking about God.[2]

In Isaiah 42: 14, we have another maternal metaphor. God says: "For a long time I have held my peace, I have kept still and restrained myself, now I will cry out like a woman in travail." The prophet Hosea described divine love in terms of the love of a husband for his wife, and of a father for his son, but paternal love has maternal traits, as the *Traduction oecuménique* of the Bible notes. Thus the Lord says: "Yet it was I who taught Ephraim to walk, I took him up in my arms"[3] and as the *Traduction oecuménique* continues, "J'étais pour eux comme ceux qui soulèvent un nourrisson contre leur joue et je lui tendais de quoi se nourrir" — "I was to them as those who held an infant against their cheek, and fed him."[4]

The Psalms[5] speak of the protection to be found in the shadow of God's wings[6], which is also a picture of motherly care. Jesus reflected this aspect of God's love when he spoke these sorrowful words: "O Jerusalem, Jerusalem, killing the prophets and stoning those who are sent to you. How often would I have gathered your children together as a hen gathers her brood under her wings, and you would not."[7]

We might add as another illustration of the motherly aspects of God's action the biblical teaching about *Sophia,* the Wisdom of

God. In the Gospel according to St Luke, Jesus says that "wisdom is justified by all her children".[8] This appears to be a reference to that personified wisdom about which much is to be found in the Book of Proverbs, and even more in the apocryphal books, *Wisdom of Solomon* and *Ecclesiasticus*. Is this *Sophia* watching over her children then a symbol of the maternal elements in the Father's love? In the sophiological tradition of many outstanding Russian philosophers and theologians, such as Soloviev, Florensky and in particular S. Boulgakov, the *Sophia* occupies a decisively important place and represents the feminine and maternal in the divine energies. According to this theology, it is "by the feminine principle of the *Sophia* that the redoubtable face of God is transformed into a human face."[9] It throws light on aspects of biblical thought neglected by Western theology, but there is a danger that it may become a theological speculation rather than an interpretation of the revelation given to us.

In the Bible, we find, then, a number of indications of maternal traits in God's love, but at the same time there is a clear reticence with regard to symbolism which could be interpreted as describing God as a mother goddess. The reason for this reserve is not far to seek. Ancient Israel was surrounded by peoples whose religious life was dominated by such goddesses, who represented the unbridled vital force of natural life. Ishtar of Babylonia, Cybele, the Great Mother of Phrygia, Astarte and Asjerah of Syria, Anath of Canaan — all represented the unceasing fertility of the earth. To worship them was to accept the supremacy of nature. This meant that sexuality was at the centre of life and that sexual rites became an important part of religious observance. Now, the unique feature of the prophetic faith described and proclaimed in the Old Testament was that it broke away from this pattern so common in the Near East. The God of Israel transcended the life of nature and sexuality. Fertility was not inherent in nature, but was a gift of God. Sacred prostitution was to be condemned, not merely because it was immoral, but because it was based on the false notion that sexuality was a divine force.

Martin Buber has given an impressive interpretation of the fight waged by the prophets against syncretistic attempts to mix the cult of Jahveh with the fertility cults. According to him, "the chief danger came from the mother goddesses,"[10] and this danger threatened not only the purity of the faith, but also the humanity of women, for in a religion in which the inherent dynamism of nature is worshipped as the force which procreates life, and always more life, women are inevitably considered as only fulfilling a sexual role. Paul D. Hanson said of the cult of the mother goddess in Babylon: "Though the dominant metaphor in this cult is feminism, it is dedicated to a view of woman which reduces her to a sex object (as the fertility plaques with their exaggerated representations of the breasts and genitalia illustrate), thereby thrusting life into a debased one-dimensionality."[11]

In the Apostolic age, mother goddesses with their fertility cult were still a force to be reckoned with. "Diana of the Ephesians", as she is called in the Act of the Apostles, was Artemis, and was acclaimed by the crowd in the theatre at a demonstration against the Christian and Jewish faiths which did not acknowledge her as a divinity, a manifestation of the Great Mother, known elsewhere as Cybele, who had a strong following in Rome.[12] In Ephesus, and in other places, St Paul had to struggle against the same naturalistic vitalism which had been rejected by the prophets of Israel.

At the same time, a new religious movement had appeared in the form of *gnosticism* which was more sophisticated and intellectually acceptable than the popular cults. It was a more dangerous challenge because it used Christian symbols, but in a context which was fundamentally different from the Christian faith. In gnostic speculation, the divine motherhood played an important role. In the eighth chapter of the Acts, Peter and John met a prophet who claimed to be "that power of God, which is called great." This man, Simon, who became known as Simon Magus, the father of gnosticism, was associated with a woman called Helena whom he called 'the Mother of all'. According to Irenaeus[13] and Justin[14] this Helena was regarded as 'the first idea', which had become incarnate in different women, such as Helen of Troy, and finally in Simon's companion who was however really a prostitute from the city of Tyre. Irenaeus added that Helena was worshipped as a goddess. In other forms of gnosticism, the divine mother is generally identified with the Holy Spirit. Thus, in the apocryphal Gospel of the Hebrews, Jesus called the Holy Spirit 'my mother'. In the Acts of Thomas, also an apocryphal book, is a conception of the Trinity in which the third person is described as the "mother, Queen of the East."[15]

Gnosticism, with its belief that the material world was evil, on the one hand produced a radical asceticism demanding the total rejection of sexuality and, on the other, a complete sexual anarchy based on the idea that what men and women did with their bodies was of no importance. Gnosticism had, as it were, a place for woman in heaven as participating in creation, and a place in hell as the temptress responsible for man's imprisonment in sexuality. It had, however, no place for her as a person, as a human being on earth. It was therefore fundamentally opposed to marriage as a life-long covenant between two persons. It is not surprising, therefore, that the early church was profoundly suspicious of all gnostic tendencies, and especially of any attempt to use feminine or maternal symbols for God.

Has this ancient story any relevance for us today? There are modern voices which claim that the time has come to rediscover the truth in the worship of the mother goddess. Thus Esther Harding, a disciple of C. G. Jung, finds in it the reflection of the depths of feminine nature, and believes that this ancient feminine principle is reasserting its power today.[16] As we have seen, D. H. Lawrence, as a modern prophet of the religion of sexual vitalism, attempted to describe, in *The Man who Died,* the victory of the mother goddess over the crucified and risen Christ. Religious philosophies based on memories of gnosticism speculate about an androgynous deity.

The paradoxical element in this situation is that precisely when the great issue is the recognition of the full human dignity of women, there is a returning interest in those ancient religious systems, in which women were not fully regarded as persons. It was because of the worship of the impersonal forces of nature that women in the ancient world did not receive their proper place. It was because of the gnostic influence in the post-Apostolic age that the confident association of men and women described in the Gospels was transformed into far less liberal relations in the church of the following centuries.[17] There is therefore good reason today to maintain a certain reserve in speaking of the motherhood of God. Theologians concerned with the liberation of women have a responsibility to identify those elements of nature worship and gnosticism which have deformed the original gospel as revealed in Jesus, and thus clarify aspects of Christian thought on the relations between men and women.

God transcends the difference of the sexes. We call him Father because Jesus has taught us to do so, and to cease so to call him is to cease to pray as Jesus enjoined us. To refuse to use any reference to God as 'He' and to choose terms such as 'the divine being' or 'the Deity' is to depersonalize God. The fatherhood of God is however not a closed or exclusive symbolism. It is open to correction, enrichment, and completion from other forms of symbol, such as 'mother', 'brother', 'sister' and 'friend'. The Bible itself gives us, as we have seen, sufficient indication of this openness to allow us to speak of maternal traits in God.

In the later history of the church, there are not many examples of the use of the image of motherhood in relation to God or to Christ. One great theologian, however, St Anselm of Canterbury, who lived in the eleventh century, wrote a prayer which became widely known, and in which divine motherhood is the central conception. He took his starting point from the passage in the Epistle to the Galatians[18] in which St Paul spoke of them as "my little children with whom I am again in travail until Christ be formed in you." St Anselm then prayed to St Paul as his "sweet nurse, sweet mother." He then asked: "And you Jesus, are you not also a mother? Are you not the mother who like a hen gathers her children under her wings?" He added: "Then both of you are mothers. Even if you are fathers, you are also mothers... Fathers by your authority, mothers by your kindness; fathers by your teaching, mothers by your mercy."[19]

While I do not suggest that prayers be addressed to St Paul, I believe that there is room in the church for the type of spiritual imagination which we find in St Anselm's prayer.

16. Emancipation is not enough

The argument that God the Father, the God of the Christian faith, is not an autocratic patriarch who keeps his children under strict control will not satisfy people today. They will wish to know whether this God desires human freedom and to question whether Christians, as people of God, are making any contribution to the liberation of human beings from the forces of oppression and domination.

These questions cannot be answered by generalities. It is not enough to point out how much the Bible has to say about freedom. The *leitmotiv* of the Old Testament is the Exodus from Egypt. Jesus came "to proclaim release to captives" and "to set at liberty those who are oppressed."[1] St Paul spoke of the "glorious liberty of the children of God."[2] Although all this is true, our modern critic is looking for evidence to show that these proclamations of freedom had concrete results in this world.

It is clear that the Christian church, at the start a very small group made up mainly of people without political or social influence, could not change overnight the ethos and structures of society, but was there at least emancipation within the Christian community?

This is not an easy question to answer, for, on the one hand, we have clear evidence that human relations were transformed within the early church and that for women, children and slaves this meant a new recognition of their human dignity. On the other hand, we know that the structures of society were not called into question, so that the family maintained its patriarchal form and the social status of women and slaves remained the same.

The reason for this apparent paradox is that the freedom of which the Bible speaks is above all the great redemptive freedom.

Human beings are victims of sin and death. Jesus came to liberate people from these arch-enemies, and the life and death struggle between God's Kingdom and the powers which enslave people is all-important, taking priority over all other struggles. In biblical terminology, therefore, freedom means the salvation of men and women, so that they may live the life to which God calls them, the life of his children. Freedom is a gift, not an achievement, and Jesus acts as God's representative in enabling people to become free. "If the Son makes you free, you will be free indeed."[3] He associates us with his own sonship, for he is "the first-born among many brethren."[4]

St Paul developed this conception of *huiethesia* or adoption, the act whereby God bestows on people the gift of being his children,[5] for people are not by nature children of God. As long as they live their self-centred lives or follow other masters, they are not yet children of God. To discover God's fatherhood, they must change the whole direction of their lives and cease to be slaves to the powers of evil. To the Romans, St Paul said that when they had learned to cry 'Abba, Father' as Jesus did, they would have become children of God in truth,[6] his heirs and fellow-heirs with Christ. He said the same to the Galatians,[7] this time illustrating his point by comparing the human being in his pre-Christian state to an orphan under care of a guardian who can receive his or her inheritance only when freed from this supervision. That moment came when God sent his Son "to redeem those that were under the law, so that we might receive adoption as sons."[8]

Here again we find the idea of emancipation expressed by St Paul, and here again he is not speaking of emancipation in the modern sense of the word. Paul is referring to the ultimate redemption of the human being, and not, in any way, of change in worldly society.

The New Testament does not deal directly and explicitly with changes needed in the structure of society. This is particularly clear when we consider the attitude of Jesus and his followers to the question of national independence. Their country had a history of heroic resistance against foreign invaders, and in Jesus' time there were courageous groups, such as the Zealots, who kept alive the spirit of the Maccabees in their fight against the occupying power of Rome. One of their centres was at Sepphoris, in the immediate neighbourhood of Nazareth. Yet the problem of national liberty

did not seem to concern Jesus and the New Testament authors.
Compared with the overwhelming experience of moving from a
meaningless world of despair to one of love and hope, the problems of being a woman, a slave, of being dependent on an earthly
father, or of living under occupation, were of secondary importance.

St Paul could therefore say to slaves in the church that their
status did not matter. "For he who was called in the Lord is a
freed man of the Lord. Likewise he who was free when called is a
slave of Christ."[9] The problems of worldly subordination and
domination had lost their acuteness as a completely new sense of
proportion entered the hearts and minds of the faithful. The distinction which mattered was not between masters and slaves, men
and women, liberated or dependent peoples, but between the life
of freedom in Christ and life under the tyranny of sin and death.

Of course, this does not mean that the emergence of the Christian community had no influence, or only a negative one, on the
process of human emancipation, for the indirect consequences of
the Christian faith in society have been very considerable.

In the first place, the message of redemption was a message concerning events in history. The Exodus was not an idea or an ideal
but a real fact. When in the *Magnificat,* the song of Mary, or the
Benedictus, the song of Zechariah, we are given the quintessence of
the great deeds of God, this again relates to deliverance from real
and visible enemies. The coming of Jesus is God's entrance into
history, and the freedom which Jesus in the Incarnation brought to
people as the flesh and bones of the Christian faith must therefore
also be freedom in history, freedom in this world.

Secondly, the freedom of which the New Testament speaks has
a cosmic dimension. The classical text is of course in the Epistle to
the Romans, where St Paul said: "Creation itself will be set free
from its bondage to decay and obtain the glorious liberty of the
children of God."[10] In the passages where St Paul spoke of
freedom in a cosmic perspective, he often referred to the powers
which dominate human life, some natural, some political and
social. People worshipped these forces which ruled the world, and
thus became their slaves. Jesus disarmed these forces and, in
triumphing over them, liberated the human person.[11] In the past,
many have considered this biblical concern with cosmic powers to
be a reflection of ancient superstitions. More recently, however,

some scholars have concluded that no reference to antique or primitive thought was intended and that these ruling powers were the systems, ideologies, 'isms', philosophies and ethical codes which had grown up and demanded of people complete adherence, making them their captives and coming between them and God. As Christians became aware that these powers did not control history, they realized that no human being should be enslaved by them. Proclaiming the victory of Christ over the powers which enslave men and women shows that these powers can be overcome, and so helps men and women in their struggle to become free.

This cosmic perspective of freedom is also clearly expressed in the many gospel stories of the casting out of demons. It has been remarked that in the oldest of the Gospels, that of St Mark, this aspect of the mission of Jesus is emphasized more strongly than his teaching. Jesus proclaimed the lordship of God and liberated people from the power of the adversary, so that in this sense, Jesus was the pioneer of human emancipation.

A third reason why the significance of Christianity for the emancipation of people must not be under-estimated is that its conception of faith is eminently dialogical. God is not an impersonal force. He calls human beings to him in order to enter into a personal relation with them. He wants them to converse with him, and that conversation is prayer. He calls his children by their names, and they respond. This kind of relationship presupposes that people *can* respond, that they are responsible beings. Should not men and women whom God treats as responsible beings, with freedom to choose to live with him or without him, therefore be treated as people who have the right and the capacity to make the social and political choices on which their earthly future and that of their children will depend?

Furthermore, the Christian faith has deeply influenced human emancipation by announcing that those who have come to know God as Father recognize one another as brothers and sisters. The impact of this insight on emancipation can be seen in the short but important letter which St Paul wrote to Philemon, whose slave, Onesimus, had run away. Onesimus had also become a convert to Christianity under Paul's influence, and Paul writes that, now that Philemon and Onesimus are both Christians, their relationship is no longer that of master and slave, but that of brothers, for they are both 'in Christ' and both acknowledge him to be their Lord. It is of interest to our theme that, while Paul made it clear that he hoped Onesimus would be released from slavery, he did not impose this decision, but left Philemon free to make up his own mind about it.

This little letter shows us that, when the new faith was taken seriously, the traditional structures of society were in fact undermined and deprived of their force. Christians were not in a position to abolish slavery. "What they could do, however, was to let the gospel through them create such relations between master and slave that the principle of one person owning and disposing of another became more and more unthinkable and obsolete."[12]

As we have mentioned above when discussing the slogan 'Everything is permitted', the problem of emancipation in the Apostolic age can be seen very clearly in the First Epistle to the Corinthians, where St Paul was writing to a group of people in a very young church, who had found his message of freedom tremendously exciting. Very concrete problems had arisen, as the new church sought to work out its style of life and make its ethical choices. These Christians were facing questions concerning sexual life, the role of women in the church, the place of spiritual gifts *(charismata)* in worship, and the attitude to be taken to customs which had their background in idolatry. It was in these matters that they expected guidance from Paul, but it is remarkable that, instead, he began his letter with a tremendous statement on the central position of the Cross in the Christian faith, and ended it with an equally impressive passage on the true meaning of the resurrection of the dead. Paul was not using theological arguments for their own sake. He was convinced that the attitude of the Corinthians to their new freedom was theologically wrong. The real issue was not whether Christians might eat the meat that had been offered to idols, or what role women might play in church life. The real issue was the true meaning of freedom. The theology of freedom professed by a considerable group among the Christians in Corinth was a gnostic theology and, as such, Paul rejected it. It was based, not on faith but on *gnosis,* which was believed to be religious knowledge, but which in fact was human speculation.[13] The main theme of this 'knowledge' was that God had already won total victory. The drama of salvation had reached its goal and the resurrection of the dead had already taken place. "The Corinthians thought that they were in the midst of the Kingdom of God"[14] so that Paul could say to them ironically: "You have come into your kingdom — and left us out."[15] It was on the basis of this tremendous misapprehension that the Corinthians made their claim to unrestricted freedom, believing that they had already become 'heavenly men', and that, because of their liberation by the gospel, they could do as they liked. The students at the Sorbonne in 1968 who wrote their belief in total emancipation on walls did not realize that they had spiritual ancestors in first century Corinth.

Paul did not ask the Corinthians to be less concerned about freedom but rather to consider whether they were talking about the true freedom which the faithful find in Christ, or about some man-made freedom. He suggested that to achieve true freedom in Christ, they must curb their enthusiasm for the lesser human freedom. They had to be sure that their freedom was really a consequence of faith, and not simply an outburst of the natural vitality of the old Adam. Paul shows us here that he was deeply concerned that the new ideas resulting from his preaching should not turn out to be another form of slavery. Again and again he warned his converts that there is a kind of freedom which is destructive because it is self-centred instead of being centred on God.

A visit to ancient Corinth throws light on the problem against which Paul was struggling, for its whole centre was occupied by houses of prostitution. It seems therefore that the entire life of the community was dedicated in theory and practice to the worship of Aphrodite, whose temple dominated the city, as its ruins do today. In the museum can be seen potsherds inscribed with the words *Aphrodites eimi,* — "I am of Aphrodite" — a phrase which Paul echoed in describing the parties in Corinth as "I am of Paul" or "I am of Christ."[16] These sherds are an indication of the fact that the overwhelming majority of the Corinthian population were men and women who 'belonged' to Aphrodite. Paul was here dealing with people of an "over-flowing religious vitality", many of whom had been attracted to the orgiastic mystery religions. "The problem of emancipation of slaves and women, though not in our modern form, had appeared on the horizon."[17]

It is easy to understand that Paul had to build a dyke against this flood of spiritual anarchy which could so easily have ruined his work in Corinth. He did this, as we have seen, in the first place by restating his theology as one wholly centred on "Jesus Christ and him crucified,"[18] a theology which is characterized by the tension between the 'already' of Christ's victory and resurrection and the 'not yet' of our condition as those whose full redemption is still to come. In this situation 'between the times', Christians are servants of Christ and therefore independent of others, a gloriously free people. In using their freedom, however, they must consider the influence of their behaviour upon their neighbours. Their freedom must not be destructive, but must 'build up'.[19] And it does build up, when it is freedom controlled by *agape,* the love which the Father pours into human hearts and which seeks not its own interest, but that of its neighbour.[20] There is therefore a tension between two attitudes in Christian life, one which seeks to make manifest the new freedom and the other which keeps that freedom under control, in recognition of the fact that Christians live in an expectant world, awaiting the coming of the Kingdom. Some believers want the church to be an experimental station, constantly testing new forms of spiritual freedom. Others want the church to refrain from such experiments and to conform to traditional standards.

In the teaching of St Paul, we find a remarkable combination of these two attitudes. In fact we find them together in one sentence when he tells the Corinthians that a woman brings shame on her head if she prays or prophesies bareheaded.[21] This shows us that Paul had accepted the new custom of letting women pray and prophesy in the church. (Although a passage in I Corinthians Chapter 14 states that women should keep silent in church,[22] this is now considered by many scholars as an interpolation dating from the period when the emphasis was again being placed on order rather than freedom and when traditional paternalism once again sought to keep women in their place.) That women may speak in church is a tremendous advance, for it would have been unthinkable in a synagogue. Paul's attitude is therefore not purely conservative. In the same sentence, however, he seeks to limit this new freedom for women, by insisting that they must cover their heads. His fear was that the new custom would lead to an enthusiasm which would be Dionysian rather than Christian. Indeed, he felt so strongly about it that he piled up a multitude of arguments against the uncovered heads of women which weakened rather than strengthened his case, appealing to Jewish tradition, [23] to a sense of decency,[24] to nature,[25] and even added a theological reflection about man as the image of God and woman as reflecting the glory of man, which is not in accordance with the story of the Creation. The apostle is here clearly under the influence of his fear of Aphrodite. His remark that for a bareheaded woman in church "it is as bad as if her head were shaved"[26] is a reference to prostitution, and, in the circumstances prevailing in the Corinth of his day, he was probably justified in his pastoral advice. It is regrettable, however, that he gave it in the form of a permanently valid norm, for that contradicts his own principle of freedom and obscures the distinction between a pastoral injunction which is valid in a given situation and a standard which is absolute for Christian life under all conditions. It is interesting to speculate whether Paul would have written in the same way if he had known that his words would reach not only a small congregation in Corinth, but also millions of people all over the world who, through the centuries, would read his words in more than a thousand different languages.

For us, the supremely important message of Paul on emancipation remains his clear statement: "For freedom Christ has set us free; stand fast therefore, and do not submit again to a yoke of slavery."[27] Paul believed in freedom, but he knew that in our human situation true freedom is always threatened by false freedom, by forces which seek to impose a new form of slavery. The danger is at its greatest when people believe that they are so magnificently free that they are in no danger of losing their freedom. Paul's teaching is echoed by Pascal when he wrote in his *Pensées:* "L'homme est ni ange ni bête." Men who behave as if they were already angels are likely to end up acting as beings who are sub-human. Shigalov, the nihilistic theorist in Dostoevsky's novel *The Possessed,* said: "My conclusion is a direct contradiction of the original idea with which I start. Starting from unlimited freedom, I arrive at unlimited despotism."[28] This is true also in Christian life. Many Corinthian and Galatian Christians, and many Christian enthusiasts and sectarians in later centuries have learned that St Paul was right.

Emancipation is not enough. What Jesus told those in his generation who listened to him is just as true today. When an unclean spirit comes out of a man it wanders over the deserts seeking a resting place, and finding none, it says: "I will go back to the home I left." So it returns and finds the house unoccupied, swept clean and tidy. Off it goes and collects seven other spirits more wicked than itself, and they all come in and settle down; and in the end the man's plight is worse than before.[29] Emancipation can rid us of spirits which oppress us, but our house must not remain unoccupied. If it is not inhabited by the Father, squatters of all kinds will take it over. "The spiritual world, like the natural, abhors a vacuum."[30]

17. Conclusion

It cannot be denied that in the course of history most efforts to assist human beings to come of age, to reach a stage where they are able to make their own decisions in life, have been met by fear or opposition from the leadership of the churches. Advocates of emancipation and their followers have nearly always been regarded as dangerous characters seeking to undermine society and the life of the church. There are, I believe, three reasons for this misunderstanding.

Firstly, church leaders feared that emancipation would inevitably lead to the disintegration of society, and in particular to the disappearance of the Christian tradition on which in the West it was based. This fear was not without justification, and it is true that the combined force of movements of emancipation in various fields has destroyed the coherence of the old *Corpus Christianum.* Individualism and pluralism have done away with that fundamental consensus of opinion on *mores,* the common criterion which also found expression in laws. Responsible church leaders have therefore often tried to apply brakes to movements of liberation from paternalistic control, the results of which they could not foresee. They failed to realize that in a number of cases such movements resulted from the application of Christian principles, and further, by their resistance, they increased the danger of a split in society, by forcing the supporters of the new movements to take a negative attitude to the traditional, patriarchal world.

In the second place, the absence of a true dialogue between the established churches and the opponents of paternalism was often due to the fact that the church leaders were generally unaware how intensely the people who desired to be treated as full members of society felt about the indignity and injustice of their position. It is astonishing how often warnings about the explosive nature of pre-revolutionary situations, whether social, national, ecclesiastical, racial, or inspired by the young, have been dismissed, even when violence or revolution was about to break out. This blindness has usually been due to a refusal to face unpleasant truths.

Thirdly, it has to be said that the unwillingness to surrender paternalistic attitudes has often been due to a desire to retain a position of domination. Sociologists tell us that paternalism "operates as a parade of benevolence which exists only so far as it is in the interest of the ruler and which requires passive acquiescence as the price of being cared for."[1] There can of course be paternalism which is an expression of genuine benevolence, but it is true that, once established as a pattern of relationship, it can very easily become a facade of good will hiding a desire for continuing domination. The unwillingness of church leaders to transform paternal structures into fraternal ones, or to give up privileged positions, has indeed often been due to a greater concern for the interests of the fathers than for those of the children.

The record of Christianity with regard to movements of liberation from paternalism in its various forms is however not wholly negative. Among those who led the struggles for emancipation there were many who did so because of and in the name of their Christian convictions. It is a striking fact that in each of the last seven centuries there have been religious movements inspired by a rediscovery of the biblical message of equality before God and justice for all which have sought to realize this vision in church and society.

In the thirteenth century, there arose a branch of the Franciscans which was influenced by Joachim di Fiore, who died in 1202, and who taught about the coming age of the Holy Spirit, when there would no longer be any need for domination in church or in society.

In the fourteenth century, John Wycliffe sent his evangelists all over England to exhort the people to choose a life of evangelical poverty, and to tell them that the "standing which a man has before God is the criterion by which his position among men must be determined."[2]

In Bohemia in the fifteenth century, John Hus, inspired by the ideas of Wycliffe, led a strong movement of protest against the clericalism and autocracy of the hierarchy. After his death a considerable number of his followers, the Taborites, interpreted the principle of the priesthood of all believers in social terms, so as to create a democratic society in which all, both men and women, would be equal.

The Reformation, in the next century, was accompanied by a number of revolutionary movements whose members, on the basis of their interpretation of the Bible, demanded that emancipation from ecclesiastical domination should be followed by the liberation of the poverty-stricken peasantry from the oppression of the nobility. One of their spokesmen was Thomas Münzer, a man in whom, as Ernst Bloch has shown,[3] the spirit of the Old Testament prophets came alive again, but who ruined his own cause by his use of violent action.

Seventeenth century England was the scene of action by many different Christian sects which had in common their rejection of the traditional order, not only in the church, but also in society. In Cromwell's army there were revolutionaries who demanded a radical renewal of society on the basis of Christian principles. The spirit of these soldiers can be gauged from the title given to one of their pamphlets: "The new Law of Righteousness: Budding forth to restore the whole Creation from the bondage and the Curse. Or a glimpse of the new Heaven and the new Earth."[4]

The eighteenth century at last saw the start of the movement to abolish slavery and the slave trade. Its exponents were Christians of different confessions, the lead having been given by the Quakers of Pennsylvania. A Quaker, John Woolman, argued that Africans were "human creatures whose souls are as precious as ours." John Wesley wrote his *Thoughts on Slavery,* and in 1787 the Evangelical Anglican, William Wilberforce, commenced his war against the slave trade in the House of Commons.

Much more could have been done by the churches in the nineteenth century, when the industrial revolution forced workers to live in intolerable conditions which they had no power to alter. At the time when Karl Marx had announced that religion was the opium of the people, the churches failed to speak out about the new abuses, as if their religion was opium which prevented them from hearing the cries of the needy. We must, however, remember those Christians who did demand that the workers should be free to defend their rights, and I would especially mention Philippe Buchez, Lamennais and other Christian Socialists in France, and

Charles Kingsley and F. D. Maurice in England, whose voices were heard as early as the Communist Manifesto of 1848, if not earlier.

In my lifetime, many Christians have made substantial contributions to emancipation. I would choose as examples the struggle for the independence of nations or races, the struggle for freedom from economic exploitation, and the struggle for a rightful place in the church for the laity, and would mention some men and women whom I have come to know personally. Men who believed profoundly in the right of all nations and peoples to independence include K. T. Paul of India, Benjamin Mays of the United States of America, Johannes Leimena of Indonesia, Eduardo Mondlane of Mozambique as well as Z. K. Matthews, Albert Luthuli, Alan Paton and Beiers Naudé of South Africa, and C. F. Andrews of the United Kingdom and India. Among those who have sought to lighten the burden of the poor I would name Toyohiko Kagawa of Japan, Barbara Ward of the United Kingdom, Helder Camara of Brazil, André Philip of France and Reinhold Niebuhr of the United States. Men and women who have sought an active role for the laity in the church include Yves Congar of France, Hendrik Kraemer of the Netherlands, John R. Mott of the United States, Reinold von Thadden of Germany and J. H. Oldham of the United Kingdom. To them I would add the names of two men who have made clear to many the significance for Christianity of the worldwide movement towards emancipation. They are Nicolas Berdyaev, who saw human destiny as the calling of humankind to realize the divine gift of freedom, and Dietrich Bonhoeffer who, in his letters from prison, challenged Christians at last to become aware of the coming of age of their contemporaries.

There is a widespread belief today that the churches are fundamentally unable to respond to people's desire to run their own life in full freedom, and as we have seen, history provides many examples which seem to justify this suspicion. Twentieth century history however leads to a less negative conclusion. Karl Barth wrote of the "turning of the churches to the world."[5] This means that the churches are learning to understand the currents in human history which lead towards emancipation. That this is a recent discovery can be seen by comparing 1848 with 1948. The year 1848 was crucial in Western history, a year of choice and decision for Europe. In the political, social and national fields, changes were seen, but in all areas the underlying issue was whether people had come of age and were to live as fully responsible human beings. At that moment, the churches were silent, or spoke out against the forces of emancipation. In Germany, the *Kirchentag*, an assembly of church leaders, proposed a day of thanksgiving for the defeat of the revolutionary tendencies, although the main issue discussed by the professors and lawyers of the Frankfurt Parliament had been nothing more radical than the creation of a constitutional monarchy. In the Netherlands, Groen van Prinsterer, the leader of the Evangelical Revival, warned against the slogan of *Liberté, Egalité, Fraternité* as a product of the secular philosophy of the times, and showed no understanding of the strong desire for greater freedom which had arisen in so many nations and classes. After 1848, Pope Pius IX, who had seemed at first to be a liberal Pope, became a crusader against modern civilization and condemned its many errors in his famous 'Syllabus'.

A hundred years later, we find a totally different atmosphere. In 1948, the First Assembly of the World Council of Churches met in Amsterdam. In its report on "The Church and the Disorder of Society" it stated: "Our churches have often given religious sanction to the special privileges of dominant classes, races and political groups, and so they have been obstacles to changes necessary in the interest of social justice and political freedom." The Assembly decided that the churches had to stand for "the Responsible Society", for "man is created and called to be a free being responsible to God and his neighbour." It was wrong to deny man the opportunity to participate in the shaping of society, "for this is the duty implied in man's responsibility towards his neighbour."

A few years later, the Second Vatican Council was held. For the first time, an Ecumenical Council elaborated a "Pastoral Constitution on the Church in the Modern World." Urging: "Let all citizens be mindful of their simultaneous right to vote freely in the interest of the common good", it declared that citizens should be allowed to participate freely and actively in establishing the constitutional basis of a political community, governing the state, determining the scope and purpose of various institutions and choosing leaders. The social order required constant improvement and great changes in society would have to take place, and God's spirit was not absent in this development.[6]

Yet it is too much to say that the age-old conflict between paternalistic church leaders and the partisans of emancipation is behind us, for the paternalistic mentality has deep roots and will not disappear overnight. Moreover, it is possible, as we have seen, to advocate emancipation in one area and to oppose it in another, and this is true also of the churches.

A new situation has however arisen. We are no longer in the period of 'the dialogue of the deaf', in which the two parties could not hear one another because the principles which they were defending were so different that they excluded any possibility of common truth.

My great-grandfather was deeply influenced by his nephew, Guillaume Groen van Prinsterer, of whom I have already spoken. As a founder of the Anti-Revolutionary Party, Groen van Prinsterer's great concern was to defend the Christian heritage of the Dutch people. He saw in the principles of the French Revolution nothing but a force for disintegration. He was not a reactionary, but his concentration on the restoration of traditional values made him overlook the values of his time. On the other hand, my grandfather, Franciscus Lieftinck, who had studied theology and become a pastor, was deeply impressed by the modernist movement in theology. He left the church, became a leading Freemason and a member of parliament, and advocated a totally secular system of education. He had come to believe that the human destiny was to be totally autonomous and to live by one's reason alone. Clearly, these two men would have been unable to find any common ground. I, on the other hand, can find common ground with both of them. I can sympathize with Groen van Prinsterer's anxiety over the disappearance of any *pouvoir spirituel,* over the lack of common convictions and the resulting incoherence of society, but I can also understand the human desire for freedom from all spiritual oppression or constraint.

So in my time has arisen this new opportunity for true dialogue, and there are a number of reasons for this. The church no longer feels secure in society. For the first time since Constantine, it has, in many countries, been the victim of attack by totalitarian ideologies or secular philosophies, and has thus a greater understanding of the cause of the oppressed. It is therefore seeking to rid itself of its triumphalism. This is a reaction not only against the spirit of Constantine, who tried to use the church as an instrument for building up political power, but also against that of Eusebius of Caesarea, who proclaimed that the victory of Constantine was the victory of the church, and applied to the church in its historical life the biblical promises concerning the final victory of the Kingdom of God. In our days, there has come a rediscovery of the eschatological dimensions of the Christian faith, of its orientation towards divine action in the future. This brings with it an awareness of the provisional, incomplete and fragile character of Christian existence, and a greater modesty about the claims of the church. At the same time, the biblical emphasis on God's care for the poor and humble has found a new echo. For men and women of our time, Jesus is he who humbled himself and brought good news to the poor, rather than being the glorious victor, as he was presented in the Baroque period, and in all triumphal art. Therefore, paternalism which has long been a feature of the churches, and which still plays a role in their life, is now challenged from within by strong counter-currents.

Further, there are signs that in the world outside the churches there is a greater readiness to take seriously what they have to say about the limitations of emancipation. An example is the widespread frustration aroused by the permissive society. Many who had longed for the glorious freedom of an era in which everything was permitted have found that it is dull, not exciting. Where there is no moral problem or spiritual conflict, life becomes colourless. Moreover, when everybody is concerned exclusively with self-expression, the world becomes increasingly incoherent, and it is impossible to undertake together the tremendous tasks on which the future of the human race depends, such as reshaping the economic order, creating a just peace and fighting ecological dangers.

The world therefore is becoming less inclined to rejoice in the decline of the father figures, realizing that to reject those who have hitherto controlled our civilization may lead to domination by dictators whose rule would even be stricter. There is therefore now the opportunity of a new dialogue between the churches and the advocates of emancipation, an opportunity which the churches must not miss. They must make it absolutely clear that they stand for the liberation of men and women from all obstacles which prevent them from living as responsible human beings. By now the churches should have learned the lesson of history, that opposition to genuine movements for emancipation is unavailing, and has done more harm than good to the cause of the Christian faith. The gravest result of such opposition has been that the gospel, a tremendous call to freedom, has come to be regarded as an instrument to prevent the full development of men and women.

At the same time, the churches must proclaim, loudly and clearly that emancipation cannot be the final goal. They must warn, as did St Paul, that a freedom which consists merely in rejecting the bounds of self-expression can easily lead to a new and more dreadful enslavement, for which there is much scope in the modern world. As to how we are to avoid this new servitude, the gospel gives a simple answer. It is by coming to the Father who allows us to live in the glorious liberty of the children of God.

The churches must furthermore make clear that emancipation in itself does not build human society. Unrelated individuals form a mass and not a community. We are entering a period in which the only solutions to the problems of peace and war, hunger and poverty and ecological danger are those inspired by self-sacrifice for the common good, and such self-sacrifice for future generations is unlikely to be made except because these generations belong as we do to the same family, of the Father in Heaven.

It is for the churches to show that to believe in the fatherhood of God according to the teaching of Jesus is not to turn to the past, but to the future. As we have seen, the misunderstanding which has caused the Christian faith to be regarded as a form of paternalism, a turning back to the spirit of ancestors, has largely been created by the churches themselves, through nostalgic attempts to return to some Golden Age, the old-time religion, the Puritan era, to mediaeval Christendom, or the early church. But the gospel of Jesus points in the opposite direction, for he has proclaimed the coming of the Kingdom in which sin and suffering will be overcome, and that Kingdom is the Kingdom of the Father.[7] He taught his disciples to pray "Our Father, Hallowed be thy name. Thy kingdom come."[8] During the Last Supper he said: "I tell you I shall not drink again of this fruit until the day when I drink it new with you in my Father's Kingdom."[9] He assured his disciples that he was going to the Father's house to prepare a place for them.[10]

Thus Jesus is the true pioneer who directs all our attention to the approaching Kingdom in which God's fatherhood will be fully revealed.[11] His followers belong to the 'cloud of witnesses' who "look forward to the city which has foundations, whose builder and maker is God",[12] and they are 'seeking a fatherland' *(patris)*.[13] They are not going backwards, they are not standing still, they are pilgrims on the road to the New Jerusalem. The announcement of the Kingdom is accompanied by signs of the new life under divine rule. Jesus summarized these signs in the words of the prophets Isaiah and Jeremiah about the time of salvation.[14] They speak of liberation, of healing, of *shalom,* the great peace, the ultimate emancipation from all oppression and alienation.

St Paul also shows that the gospel of God's fatherhood embraces the total history of salvation and the whole life of creation. For the moment, we 'groan inwardly', as we wait for our adoption as children of God, but we look forward 'with eager longing' to the time when the full meaning of God's fatherhood will be revealed and we shall obtain "the glorious liberty of the children of God."[15]

In our great struggles for emancipation what is most needed are men and women who have in their hearts this eager longing for the life of true freedom in the Kingdom of the Father, and who express this in word and deed.

We have thus seen that there are three ways of responding to the urge for emancipation. There is first of all the attempt to deny its validity. This is at best based on the fear that emancipation will lead to the weakening of the fragile fabric of society, but it is also often accompanied by the selfish desire to maintain the privileges of the dominating class, group, nation or sex. This resistance can slow up the historical process, but where it takes the form of complete blindness to the just claims of the oppressed or dominated, it becomes a danger for all society, because it makes impossible a non-violent and orderly transition towards freedom.

The second response to the widespread desire for emancipation is to treat it as a panacea or universal remedy. Those who take this view feel that the problems created by emancipation must be solved by more emancipation. It is strange that, although the world has now experienced emancipation in many areas, there are still innumerable people who have the childish faith that emancipated men and women will automatically become responsible and reliable participants in a new society based on justice for all. They forget that, while emancipation makes responsible life possible, it also opens the way to egocentric, self-assertive life. The autonomy thus established can become the denial of all social bonds and lead to that anarchy which already characterizes so much of our modern living.

The third way of responding is to see emancipation as a necessary stage in the transition to a more mature form of culture. Through this, human beings can decide in full freedom and without constraint how they will use their lives. Emancipation is seen not to be an end in itself. The mature human being is one who has passed through emancipation to personal commitment, that is to the conscious choice of the truth or cause, worthy to be served.

One of the most tragic aspects of our time is that masses of people now have as their one principle "I do not want to be committed." In rejecting commitment, these people are thrown back on to the meagre resources of their own ego. Their great need is to discover that there is a commitment which is not enslavement but fulfilment, the commitment to the Father we come to know through Christ Jesus.

Notes

Chapter 3

1. RSV Ex. 21: 7.
2. Juvencius.
3. RSV Mark 7: 5.
4. Horace, *Odes*, IV, 15.
5. *Ibid.*, IV, 5.
6. Augustine, *City of God*, XIX: 16.
7. Thomas Aquinas, *De Regimine Principum*, I: 1.
8. Jean Calvin, *Institutes of the Christian Religion*, II: 8: 38.
9. Dietrich Bonhoeffer, *Fragmente aus Tegel*, Kaiser, Munich, 1978, p. 171.
10. Dietrich Bonhoeffer, *Letters and Papers from Prison*, SCM, London, 1976, p. 295.

Chapter 4

1. Suetonius, *The Twelve Caesars*, Augustus 58.
2. *Ibid.*, Tiberius 67.
3. Bossuet, quoted by Paul Hazard, *La crise de la conscience européenne*, Boivin, Paris, 1935, pp. 279 ff.
4. Louis Bertrand, *Louis XIV*, Fayard, Paris, 1923, p. 385.
5. Bossuet, quoted by Hazard, *op. cit.*, p. 285.
6. Voltaire, *Poème sur la loi naturelle*, 1751.
7. Heinrich Heine, *Zeitgedichte* (Poems of the Time):

> Wir nennen sie Väter, und Vaterland
> Benennen wir dasjenige Land
> Das erbeigentümlich gehört den Fürsten
> Wir lieben auch Sauerkraut mit Würsten.

Wenn unser Vater spazierengeht
Ziehn wir den Hut mit Pietät;
Deutschland, die fromme Kinderstube,
Ist keine römische Mördergrube.

8. Dostoevsky, *Politische Schriften*, Piper, Munich, 1920, p. xlvi.

Chapter 5

1. *Evangelisches Soziallexikon*, Kreuz Verlag, Stuttgart, 1954, p. 574.
2. Jean Calvin, *Commentary on Ephesians*, 6: 7.
3. Jean Calvin, *Institutes of the Christian Religion*, II: 8: 36.
4. Martin Luther, *Warning Concerning Peace in Answer to the Twelve Articles of the Peasants.*
5. Calvin, see André Bieler, *La pensée économique et sociale de Calvin*, Georg, Geneva, 1959, p. 305.
6. Calvin, see Bieler, *op. cit.,* p. 355.
7. R. H. Tawney, *Religion and the Rise of Capitalism*, Penguin, London, 1940, p. 171.
8. *The Works of John Locke*, London, 1727, Vol. II, p. 193.
9. Arthur Young, see Tawney, *op. cit.,* p. 241.
10. Booker T. Washington, *Up from Slavery*, Oxford University Press, 1945, p. 16.
11. J. A. Schumpeter, *Capitalism, Socialism and Democracy*, Allen & Unwin, London, 1947, p. 8.
12. H. R. Holst, *Wordingen*, Brusse, Rotterdam, 1949, p. 110.
13. Holst, *op. cit.,* p. 111.
14. Karl Marx, *Critique of Philosophy of Law*, Oeuvres Philosophiques, Costes, Paris, 1927.
15. Peter Berglar, *Die gesellschaftliche Evolution der Menschheit*, Bibliotheca Christiana, Bonn, 1965, p. 215.
16. Holst, *op. cit.,* pp. 137 and 234.
17. J. H. Oldham and W. A. Visser 't Hooft, *The Church and its Function in Society*, Allen & Unwin, London, 1937, p. 180.

Chapter 6

1. Erasmus, *A Treatise on Missions*, 1535.
2. Jawaharlal Nehru, *The Discovery of India*, Signet, Calcutta, 1946, p. 329.

3. Seton Kerr, see Nehru, *op. cit.*, p. 387.
4. Georges Goyau, *Idée de la patrie et l'humanitairisme*, Perrin, Paris, 1913, p. 272.
5. James Bryce, see Barbara Tuchman, *The Proud Tower*, Bantam, New York, 1972, p. 172.
6. Tuchman, *op. cit.*, p. 185.
7. R. Tagore, see Nehru, *op. cit.*, pp. 380-381.
8. C. F. Andrews, see J. N. Farquhar, *Modern Religious Movements in India*, McMillan, New York, 1919, p. 350.
9. John Morley, see Nehru, *Autobiography*, Bodley Head, London, 1936, p. 500.
10. *Christ and Students of the East*, WSCF, Geneva, 1933, p. 105.
11. Nehru, *The Discovery of India*, p. 656.
12. Report: Bloemfontein Congress, p. 120.

Chapter 7

1. Henriette Visser 't Hooft-Boddaert, "Is There a Woman's Problem?", *The Student World*, First Quarter, 1934.
2. Henriette Visser 't Hooft-Boddaert, "Eve, Where Art Thou?", *The Student World*, Third Quarter, 1936, p. 208. The correspondence between Henriette Visser 't Hooft and Karl Barth has been published in "Eva, wo bist Du?", Burckhardthaus, Berlin, 1981. See also: Susannah Herzel, *A Voice for Women*, WCC, Geneva, 1981.
3. Claire Tomalin, *The Life and Death of Mary Wollstonecraft*, Mentor Books, The New American Library Inc., 1976, p. 103.
4. Frances Willard, see Gilbert Seldes, *The Stammering Century*, John Day, New York, 1928, p. 264.
5. H. G. Wells, *Experiment in Autobiography*, McMillan, New York, 1934.
6. Emma Goldman, see L. Horowitz, *The Anarchists*, Dell, New York, 1964, pp. 267-277.
7. Simone de Beauvoir, *Le deuxième sexe*, Gallimard, Paris, 1949, p. 228.
8. Michael Bakunin & Masaryk, *The Spirit of Russia*, quoted in Horowitz, *The Anarchists*, Dell, New York, 1964, p. 469.
9. Percy Bysshe Shelley, *Notes on "Queen Mab"*, (1813), Complete Poetical Works, Oxford University Press, London, 1909.
10. Dietrich Bonhoeffer, *Letters and Papers from Prison*, SCM, London, 1976, p. 130. The translation given in this book "to *present afresh* middle-class life" is incorrect. The original text has *Rehabilitierung*.

That Bonhoeffer's intention was indeed to rehabilitate bourgeois family-life is shown in the fragments of the novel written in prison: *Fragmente aus Tegel,* Kaiser Verlag, Munich, 1978.

11. Karl Marx, *Oeuvres philosophiques,* Costes, Paris, 1927, Tome I, pp. 102 and 105.
12. Mary Daly, *Beyond God the Father, Toward a Philosophy of Women's Liberation,* Boston, Beacon Press, 1973, p. 190.
13. Paul Evdokimov, *La femme et le salut du monde,* Casterman, Paris, 1958, p. 266.
14. Catherina Halkes, in *Deutsches Allgemeines Sonntagsblatt,* 23 March 1980.
15. Catherina Halkes, *Wenn Frauen ans Wort kommen,* Burckhardthaus, Berlin, 1979, p. 36.
16. Karl Heim, *Glaube und Denken,* Furche, Berlin, 1931, p. 405.
17. Karl Barth, *Church Dogmatics,* II, 1:331.
18. Barth, *op. cit.,* III:2.
19. Barth, *op. cit.,* III:4.

Chapter 8

1. Translation: "In our time, you played the fool with crowds of wild young people, who were diabolically gifted."
2. Priscilla Robertson, *Revolutions of 1848,* Harpers, New York, 1952, p. 250.
3. Michael Bakunin & Masaryk, *The Spirit of Russia,* quoted in Horowitz, *The Anarchists,* Dell, New York, 1964, p. 468.
4. Quoted by Georg Merz, *Zwischen den Zeiten,* Vol. V, 1924.
5. W. A. Visser 't Hooft, "The Youth of 1927 and the Youth of 1932' *World's Youth,* October 1932.
6. Karl Shapiro, see *The Anarchists,* ed. by Horowitz, Dell, New York, 1964, p. 573.
7. Theodore Roszak, *The Making of a Counter-Culture,* Doubleday, New York, 1969, p. 34.

Chapter 9

1. Pope Gregory VII, see Bettenson, *Documents of the Christian Church,* pp. 147 and 153.
2. *Kirchengeschichtliches Lesebuch,* Mohr, Tübingen, 1915, p. 145.
3. Baron Friedrich von Hügel, *Essays and Addresses on the Philosophy of Religion,* Dent, London, 1921, pp. 233-234.

4. Hügel, *op. cit.,* Second Series, p. 17.
5. W. R. Hogg, *Ecumenical Foundations,* Harper, New York, 1952, p. 81.
6. Second Vatican Council, "Decree on the Bishops' Pastoral Office," No. 16.

Chapter 10

1. RSV, Deut. 6: 6-7.
2. RSV, Ps. 78: 5-6.
3. RSV, Matt. 5: 12.
4. RSV, Matt. 22: 34-40.
5. See Rom. 13: 8-10, Gal. 5: 14.
6. See I Cor. 12: 31.
7. See Rom. 5: 5.
8. See Gal. 3: 24.
9. See I Cor. 9: 21.
10. See I Cor. 14: 34.
11. See Acts 21: 24-26.
12. See Barnabas 2: 6.
13. See Gal. 5: 1.
14. See I Cor. 6: 12 and 10: 23.
15. Irenaeus, *Adversus Haereses,* I: 6.
16. Clement of Alexandria, *On Marriage,* 4: 30.
17. Jacob Burckhardt, *Kultur der Renaissance in Italien,* Kröner, Leipzig, 1919, 12th edition II: 122.
18. Jean Calvin, *Institutes of the Christian Religion,* IV: 12: 1.
19. Translation: "Honour is due to kings, they do whatever pleases them. Louis."
20. A remarkably clear account of the influence of "Le Neveu de Rameau" has been given by Lionel Trilling in *Sincerity and Authenticity,* Harvard, Cambridge, 1973, pp. 27-47.
21. Denis Diderot, *Rameau's Nephew,* Penguin Classics, pp. 83-84, trans. Tancock, 1966.
22. Werner Elert, *Der Kampf um das Christentum,* Beck, Munich, 1921, p. 210.
23. Dominique Arban, *Dostoevsky par lui-même,* Seuil, Paris, 1962, p. 130-131.
24. *Ibid.* p. 129.
25. Friedrich Nietzsche, *Genealogie der Moral,* III: 24.

26. Karl Jaspers, *Nietzsche,* de Gruyter, Berlin, 1950, p. 233.
27. Anatole France, *Histoire comique,* Calmann-Levy, Paris, 1924, p. 6.
28. Hermann Hesse, *Demian,* Suhrkamp, 1972, p. 146.
29. Albert Camus, *L'homme revolté,* Gallimard, Paris, 1951, p. 94.
30. Trans.: "It would reduce the earth to rubble and swallow up the world in a yawn — It is Boredom."

Chapter 11
1. B. Spinoza, *Ethica,* V: 17, 19.
2. Voltaire, *Lettres philosophiques.*
3. Voltaire, *Poème sur le désastre de Lisbonne* (1756).
4. William Blake, *Songs of Innocence — the Divine Image.*
5. William Blake, see Bronowski, *William Blake,* Penguin, London, 1954, p. 188.
6. Friedrich Nietzsche, *Genealogie der Moral,* Second Dissertation, No. 22.
7. Karl Marx, *Oeuvres philosophiques,* Costes, Paris, 1927, Tome I, p. 84.
8. Trans.: "We leave Heaven to angels and sparrows."
9. P. J. Proudhon, in Löwith, *Wereldgeschiedenis,* Aula, Utrecht, 1960, p. 63.
10. Michael Bakunin, quoted in Camus, *L'homme revolté,* Gallimard, Paris, 1951, p. 192.
11. Albert Einstein, quoted in Mitscherlich, *Auf dem Weg zur vaterlosen Gesellschaft,* Piper, Munich, 1965, p. 391.
12. Albert Camus, *op. cit.,* p. 179.
13. André Gide, *The Parable of the Prodigal Son.*

Chapter 12
1. Second Vatican Council, "Pastoral Constitution on the Church in the Modern World (Gaudium et Spes)," paras. 55 and 10.
2. H. G. Wells, *A Short History of the World,* Tauchnitz, Leipzig, 1923, p. 229.
3. Charles Malik, "Human Rights and Religious Liberty", *The Ecumenical Review,* Summer 1949, No. 4, p. 404.
4. Michael Bakunin, quoted by Horowitz, *The Anarchists,* Dell, New York, 1964, p. 133.
5. D. H. Lawrence, *The Plumed Serpent,* Knopf, New York, 1926.
6. Herbert Marcuse, *Eros and Civilization,* Sphere Books, London, 1969, pp. 32, 85 and 76.

Chapter 13

1. Lord Rosebery, quoted by W. T. Stead, "Lest We Forget", *Review of Reviews*, London, 1901, p. 36.
2. Reinhold Niebuhr, *Faith and History*, Scribner's, New York, 1949, p. 6.
3. A. de Tocqueville, *Democratie en Amérique*, I, p. 8.
4. Thomas Carlyle, quoted by W. T. Stead, *op. cit.*, p. 36.
5. Jacob Burckhardt, quoted by Löwith, *Wereldgeschiedenis*, Aula, Utrecht, 1960, p. 22.
6. Jacob Burckhardt, *Weltgeschichtliche Betrachtungen*, Kröner, Stuttgart, 1955, p. 136.
7. Ernest Renan, *L'avenir de la science, Pensées de 1848*, Paris, 1890.
8. H. G. Wells, *A Short History of the World*, Tauchnitz, Leipzig, 1923, p. 259.
9. H. G. Wells, *The Mind at the End of its Tether*, pp. 4-5.
10. Reinhold Niebuhr, *Faith and History*, Scribners, New York, 1949, p. 7.
11. Martin Buber, *Paths in Utopia*, Routledge & Kegan Paul, 1949, p. 123.
12. Roger Garaudy, *L'alternative*, Laffont, Paris, 1972, p. 44.
13. Theodore Roszak, *The Making of a Counter Culture*, Doubleday, New York, 1969, p. 141.
14. Rudolf Eucken, *Geistige Strömungen der Gegenwart*, Veit, Leipzig, 1916, p. 291.
15. T. S. Eliot, *The Idea of a Christian Society*, Faber, London, 1939, p. 15.
16. Friedrich Gentz, quoted by Egon Friedell, *Kulturgeschichte der Neuzeit*, Deutscher Taschenbuch Verlag, Munich, 1976, p. 972.
17. Pope Pius IX, *Syllabus of Errors*.
18. Archbishop D'Souza, *Die Autorität der Freiheit*, Kösel, Munich, 1967, Vol. III: 33.
19. Henry Picker, *Hitler's Tischgespräche*, Seewald, Stuttgart, 1976, pp. 214, 488, 301.
20. Dietrich Bonhoeffer, *Gesammelte Schriften*, Kaiser, Munich, 1958, pp. 356-371.
21. Walter Lipgens, *Europa-Föderationspläne der Widerstandsbewegungen*, Oldenbourg, Munich, 1968, pp. 392-396.
22. Reinhold Niebuhr, *Faith and History*, Scribners, New York, 1949, p. 232.
23. Peter Berglar, *Die Gesellschaftliche Evolution der Menschheit*, Bibliotheca Christiana, Bonn, 1965, pp. 125, 291, 298.

Chapter 14

1. RSV, Luke 2:49.
2. See Mark 14:36.
3. Joachim Jeremias, *Die Gleichnisse Jesu,* Vandenhoeck & Ruprecht, Gottingen, 1952, 2nd ed., p. 137.
4. Edward Schillebeeckx, *Jesus: an Experiment in Christology,* Collins, London, 1979, p. 266.
5. RSV, Matt. 18:3.
6. Jeremias, *op. cit.,* p. 137.
7. Schillebeeckx, *op. cit.,* p. 266.
8. Hamerton-Kelly, in *Concilium 163,* 1981, French edition, p. 149.
9. Mark 10:2-4.
10. RSV, John 4:27.
11. Karl Barth, *Kirchliche Dogmatik,* iii, 4: 279.
12. RSV, Luke 2:51.
13. Mark 10:19.
14. RSV, Mark 3:33.
15. Mark 3:31-35; see also Matt. 12:46 and Luke 8:19.
16. RSV, Mark 3:35.
17. RSV, Matt. 23:9.
18. See Luke 8:13, Mark 15:41.
19. See Luke 10:39, John 4:7-26.
20. Deut. 24:1.
21. Matt. 19:8.
22. K. Stendahl, as quoted in *Peake's Commentary,* Nelson, London, 1962.
23. Mark 7:5.
24. Matt. 20:1-16.
25. Matt. 20:15
26. RSV, Luke 15:29.
27. Deut. 21:18-21.
28. RSV, John 8:35-36.
29. RSV, John 15:15.
30. RSV, Matt. 4:3.
31. RSV, Matt. 4:6.
32. Luke, 17:20.
33. RSV, Matt. 11:25; see also Luke 10:27.

34. Mark 10: 42.
35. John 13: 3-5.
36. RSV, John 3: 16.
37. RSV, Rom. 8: 32.
38. RSV, Phil. 2: 5-11.
39. Hendrik Berkhof, *Het Christelijk Geloof,* Callenbach, Nijkerk, 1973, p. 147.
40. RSV, Matt. 21: 5.
41. Martin Luther, see Douglas John Hall, *Lighten Our Darkness,* Westminster Press, Philadelphia, 1976, p. 119.
42. F. Dostoevsky, *The Brothers Karamazow,* Book V, Chapter V.
43. Dietrich Bonhoeffer, *Letters and Papers from Prison,* enlarged edition, SCM, London, 1976, p. 361.
44. Claude Geffré, *Concilium 163,* 1981, French edition, p. 76.
45. Hans Küng, On Being a Christian, Collins, London, 1977, p. 312.

Chapter 15
1. See *The Ecumenical Review,* October 1975, p. 387.
2. See *Expositor's Bible,* The Book of Isaiah I-XXXIX, p. 245, and the Book of Isaiah, XXXX-LXVI, p. 385, Armstrong, New York, 1896.
3. Hos. 11: 3.
4. Hos. 11: 4.
5. See Deut. 32: 11.
6. Ps. 17: 8, 36: 7, 57: 2, 63: 7.
7. RSV, Luke 13: 34.
8. RSV, Luke 7: 35.
9. Paul Evdokimov, *La femme et le salut du monde,* Casterman, Paris, 1958, p. 199.
10. Martin Buber, *The Prophetic Faith,* Harper, New York, 1949, p. 121.
11. Paul D. Hanson, *The Ecumenical Review,* October 1975, p. 318.
12. Acts, chap. 19.
13. Irenaeus, *Adversus Haereses,* I: 23.
14. Apology I: 26.
15. Acts of Thomas 111.
16. Esther Harding, *Woman's Mysteries, Ancient and Modern,* Longmans Green, London, 1936.
17. Klaus Thraede, *Freunde in Christus werden,* Burckhardthaus, Berlin, 1977, pp. 129-131.

18. Gal. 7: 19.
19. St Anselm of Canterbury, *The Prayers and Meditations of St Anselm* (translated by Ward, Benedicta), Penguin Classics, 1973, pp. 152-155.

Chapter 16

1. RSV, Luke 4: 18.
2. RSV, Rom. 8: 21.
3. RSV, John 8: 36.
4. RSV, Rom. 8: 29.
5. See Rom. 8: 15 and 23, Gal. 4: 6, Eph. 1: 5.
6. See Rom 8: 15-16.
7. Gal. 4: 6-7.
8. RSV, Gal. 4: 1-7.
9. RSV, 1 Cor. 7: 22.
10. RSV, Rom. 8: 21.
11. See Col. 2: 15.
12. C. F. B. Moule, in *Peake's Commentary,* Nelson, London, 1962, p. 995.
13. See 1 Cor. 8: 23.
14. Julius Schniewind, *Nachgelassene Schriften,* Töpelmann, Berlin, 1952, p. 124.
15. NEB, 1 Cor. 4: 8.
16. RSV, 1 Cor. 1: 12.
17. Ernst Käsemann, *Der Ruf der Freiheit,* Mohr, Tübingen, 1968, pp. 88-89.
18. RSV, 1 Cor. 2: 2.
19. See 1 Cor. 10: 23.
20. See 1 Cor. 13: 4 and Phil. 2: 4.
21. RSV, 1 Cor. 11: 5.
22. RSV, 1 Cor. 14: 34-35.
23. RSV, 1 Cor. 11: 2.
24. RSV, 1 Cor. 11: 13.
25. RSV, 1 Cor. 11: 14.
26. NEB, 1 Cor. 11: 5.
27. RSV, Gal. 5: 1.
28. F. Dostoevsky, *The Possessed,* Modern Library, 1936, p. 409.
29. NEB, Matt. 12: 43-45.
30. G. B. Caird.

Chapter 17

1. Richard Sennett, *Authority*, Secker and Warburg, London, 1980, p. 131.
2. Parkes Cadman, *The Three Religious Leaders of Oxford*, McMillan, New York, 1916, p. 66.
3. Ernst Bloch, in *Die Wahrheit der Ketzer*, Stuttgart-Berlin, 1968, p. 111.
4. Ed. Bernstein, *Sozialismus und Demokratie in der grossen Englischen Revolution*, Dietz, Stuttgart, 1908, p. 134.
5. Karl Barth, *Hinwendung zur Welt* — *Kirchliche Dogmatik*, iv.:3, p. 21.
6. Second Vatican Council, "Pastoral Constitution on the Church in the Modern World (Gaudium et Spes)", paras. 28 and 75.
7. See Matt. 13: 43.
8. RSV, Luke 11: 2, cf. Matt. 6: 9-10.
9. RSV, Matt. 26: 29.
10. RSV, John 14: 2-3.
11. See Heb. 12: 2.
12. RSV, Heb. 11: 10.
13. See Heb. 11: 14, *Patris* in the Greek.
14. RSV, Luke 4: 18-19 and Luke 7: 22.
15. RSV, Rom. 8: 18-23.